IT TAKES A NATION

HOW STRANGERS BECAME FAMILY
IN THE WAKE OF HURRICANE KATRINA

The Story of MoveOn.org Civic Action's HurricaneHousing.org

EDITED BY LAURA DAWN

PHOTOGRAPHS BY C. B. SMITH

FOREWORD BY SENATOR BARACK OBAMA

EARTH AWARE

EARTH AWARE

Earth Aware Editions
17 Paul Drive
San Rafael, CA 94903
www.earthawareeditions.com
415.526.1370
For orders, call 800-688-2218
or visit www.earthawareeditions.com

Library of Congress Cataloging-in-Publication Data available.

ISBN 1-932771-86-7

Palace Press International, in association with Global ReLeaf, will plant two
trees for each tree used in the manufacturing of this book. Global ReLeaf
is an international campaign by American Forests, the nation's oldest
nonprofit conservation organization and a world leader in planting trees for
environmental restoration.

10 9 8 7 6 5 4 3 2 1

BOOK CREDITS
Compiled and Edited by Laura Dawn

Photographs by C. B. Smith
Interview Team:
Annie Nocenti, Daron Murphy, Pete Nelson, Mark Huntley, & Laura Dawn

Editing Team:
Laura Dawn, Sabin Streeter, Annie Nocenti, Pete Nelson, Daron Murphy

Copy Editor: Cree McCree

Earth Aware Editions
Publisher and Creative Director: Raoul Goff
Executive Directors: Michael Madden, Peter Beren
Acquiring Editor: Lisa Fitzpatrick
Art Director: Iain Morris
Studio Production Manager: Noah Potkin
Designer: Andrew Ogus
Project Editor: Emilia Thiuri
Production Manager: Lisa Bartlett

Printed in China by Palace Press International
www.palacepress.com

CONTENTS

HOW STRANGERS BECAME FAMILY
IN THE WAKE OF HURRICANE KATRINA
By Senator Barack Obama

Over one-and-a-half centuries ago, it was famously observed that, "America is great because Americans are good."

In the days following Hurricane Katrina, this greatness was called into question. Our government's slow and stumbling response left people across the country wondering why we couldn't seem to save a major American city from drowning. We witnessed firsthand the poverty and hopelessness that had battered the residents of New Orleans long before Katrina ever did.

And yet, as is often the case during times of great tragedy and despair, it was the fundamental decency of the American people that quickly shone through. An outpouring of compassion and sacrifice saved the stranded and housed the homeless and gave hope to the Gulf Coast's survivors.

On any ordinary day, I know it seems difficult to detect this spirit of selflessness at work. We turn on the news or open the paper and see stories of greed and corruption alongside tales of want and despair, hunger and poverty. The stories may give us pause or make us angry, but inevitably most of us soon return to our busy, orderly lives.

Then an event like Katrina happens—a crisis that shakes off our complacency and refuses to let us ignore the suffering in our midst. Suddenly, we're reminded of how very fragile life is.

We're reminded of how there's nothing inevitable about being able to turn on the tap and fill up a glass of water or returning to a dry house with a sturdy roof. We realize there's nothing inevitable about the food we eat, the clothes on our backs, or the medicine that keeps us alive. And we understand there's nothing inevitable about leaving our children in the morning and expecting that we'll see them again at night.

As we were faced with life's fragility in the days following Katrina—as we were reminded that everything we take for granted is not always granted to everybody—I think that Americans everywhere began to imagine what it would be like to live in New Orleans or Biloxi or Gulfport, what it would be like to see the place you grew up lying in ruin, what it would be like to see your childhood neighborhoods underwater, to see your home and your possessions and everything you've worked for washed away without warning or reason.

I think that moment of imagining and the action that followed is when we became a national community again. It's when people from Chicago and Houston, Tacoma and Charleston, Boston and Denver picked up their phones and called a charity, packed up their cars and headed to the Gulf, or readied the extra bedroom for the arrival of complete strangers who could stay as long as they wanted.

Most offered this help not out of pity or guilt, but empathy—that simple, profound notion that I can see the world through another person's eyes. That allows us, just for a moment, to imagine standing in someone else's shoes.

From the beginning, this idea has been at the very center of the American experience—that despite our melting pot of races and backgrounds and beliefs, we still feel a responsibility toward each other. That there are some things we just can't do on our own. It's what brought together white and black, rich and poor to march together and fight together for civil rights. It's what has sent soldier after soldier to risk their lives to save those of people they never met. And it's what caused the Americans in this book to follow the simple message heard in churches and mosques, synagogues and Sunday schools: to treat your neighbor as you would want to be treated yourself.

There's no way of knowing how long the surge of empathy that followed Katrina will last. In fact, just months after the hurricane hit, it's already become easier for the media and the public to ignore the stories we're hearing about survivors still pleading with the government for trailers and food stamps. But the goodness detailed in *It Takes a Nation*—goodness we have seen and hopefully performed ourselves—proves that in this country still lies the capacity for greatness. The oral histories in this collection show everyday heroes at work, as we see MoveOn members and countless other Americans welcome over 30,000 strangers into their homes as neighbors and friends. It shows the power this online community has to strengthen our national community, and it calls each of us to do what we can to follow this heartfelt example.

In the end, we will rise or fall as a nation depending on our ability to harness that spirit to do and care for others—not just in response to a hurricane or a terrorist attack or a tsunami—but in response to the everyday Katrinas so many of our neighbors quietly and desperately live with. It's not as easy when the crisis isn't right in front of our faces, but that doesn't mean it's not there, and it doesn't mean we can turn inward and ignore it.

America is great because Americans are good. It is a message you'll recognize on the pages of this book and one I hope we all try to live in the months and years to come. ⇨

HURRICANE HOUSING.ORG: HOW IT ALL STARTED

By Eli Pariser, Executive Director, MoveOn.org Civic Action

When I dialed onto our 4 p.m. team phone call the afternoon of Wednesday, August 31st, it was only natural to start with the disaster that was rapidly unfurling in New Orleans. We knew MoveOn members would want to help. But beyond a donation to the Red Cross, we weren't sure how they could.

We tossed ideas around for a little while: New Orleans-themed house parties to raise money, with gumbo? A website to gather frequent flier miles so that evacuees could reach their friends and family?

Ben Brandzel, our Advocacy Director, jumped in: "There's a housing crisis, right? And we've got three million members. Some of them, I'm sure, would offer housing. What if we set up a website where folks can offer and find housing?"

At first, I thought HurricaneHousing might be a mistake. Would folks really open their homes to complete strangers? I wanted to believe they would, but with CNN's news ticker full to capacity with reports of homicides and rapes, I didn't know.

We went ahead anyway. What else could we do? Good people were suffering, and getting them into safe housing as soon as possible had to be our first priority. Adam Ruben, our Political Director, began making calls to relief organizations. Ben began work on an email message to our members and Organizing Director Justin Ruben began designing the system itself.

Around 10 p.m. that night, Justin finished a prototype version of the site, and passed it off to Randall Farmer and Patrick Kane—two crack technologists who would spend the early hours of the morning turning the idea into a working program.

At 3:05 a.m., early Thursday morning, Ben finished the email message to send to our members. It said: "Today, tens of thousands are being bused to a stadium in Houston, where they may wait for months. Almost 80,000 are competing for area shelters, and countless more are in motels, their vehicles or wherever they can find. But if you've got a spare room, extra bed or even a decent couch—you may be able to help."

And at 11:12 a.m—about seventeen hours after the idea had emerged—our email went out to three million MoveOn members.

Offers of housing were beginning to trickle in—not many, but a few. We decided that if folks offered a thousand beds, that would justify the energy we were putting into the project. But would we get there?

Laura Dawn, who edited this book, began reaching out to folks in the entertainment world. By 4:35 p.m. on Thursday, R.E.M. and Pearl Jam had linked to the HurricaneHousing site. At 5:06, Moby, the Roots, and MTV joined them. Actors John Cusack, Tim Robbins and Rosie Perez dropped everything to quickly record Public Service Announcements to get the word out about the website on TV and radio.

MeetUp highlighted the site to its members. TrueMajority, another online advocacy group, sent the link out to folks Friday morning. JohnKerry.com highlighted the site. MySpace, the social networking website, offered us a free full-page advertisement to help attract hosts in the Southeast, where most of the evacuees were stranded.

Gannett News Service put out a story about the initiative. "Within hours of inception, www.hurricanehousing.org

had dozens of housing postings. A college student in Starkville, Mississippi had room for two non-smokers. A family in Navarre, Florida could take two children who could go to public schools there." Radio stations and TV stations began running the URL on the air, encouraging evacuees in search of housing—and potential hosts—to go sign up.

The number of postings was quickly increasing. Only five hours after we'd launched the email, a few thousand people had offered room for folks to stay. The next morning, 8,777 had offered 30,021 slots. In the critical states surrounding Louisiana, folks were offering beds at a rapidly increasing rate: 1,156 from 6 a.m. to 7 a.m. on Friday, over 2,000 from 7 a.m. to 8 a.m.

They were coming from all over the country: a thousand places to stay in Austin, Texas, 1,650 in Atlanta, Georgia, 1,196 in Denver, even a thousand up in Boston. People from all walks of life were opening their homes—rich and poor, Democrats and conservative Republicans who disclaimed MoveOn politics but were grateful for the opportunity to help anyway.

As the offers kept pouring in, we realized our primary challenge was swiftly changing from supply to demand. There were hundreds of thousands of folks who needed housing—but how to reach them?

In the makeshift shelters where most evacuees were staying, few people had access to the web. Justin and Matt Ewing, one of our key field organizers, had an idea: create an 800 number to allow evacuees to "search" the listings by phone.

On Friday, a little over twenty-four hours after the site had launched, folks had posted space for 51,000 people to stay, and we started getting the first reports of successful connections.

Leon, an attorney in Atlanta, took in ten people who began arriving Friday night. Kim, in Ann Arbor, Michigan, heard about the site on the radio, signed up and was preparing to host a family on Monday. A day later, there were over 60,000 places to stay offered by 26,196 individuals. In the end, there would be over 80,000 slots offered.

At 7:52 p.m. on Saturday, the toll-free number went live. By Tuesday, the operators were taking thousands of calls a day from evacuees who heard about it from Red Cross caseworkers, TV and radio stations, and word of mouth in the shelters where folks were staying. Even actor Sean Penn went on Larry King Live and interrupted the interview every thirty seconds to repeat the 800 number.

When folks started emailing us to tell us that the service was working, we could have wept.

> We were a bit unsure about letting complete strangers in our home, but my husband and I both felt that if we opened our home in the right spirit, God would bless us in return—and He has done so already! We were blessed to house a young couple, like ourselves, whose house was completely destroyed by Katrina. We have nothing but good things to say about them. They are RESILIENT. Everyday, they are out the door trying to make things happen for them here in Dallas. They show us that life really is about facing challenges head on. Amongst all their misfortune, they still have time to smile.
>
> —James & Tiffany, Dallas, Texas

> I am on HUD and I had to get permission from the housing authority to house evacuees. My story is that the poor is helping the poor. I don't have a dime so I couldn't help that

way but I do have a roof over my head and a freezer full of food that I was willing to share in order to help out. I am glad that I could help.
    —*Bryan, Hot Springs, Arkansas*

Over the following weeks, around 30,000 people found a place to stay in someone else's home. Some provided a bed to sleep in for one night between point A and point B. Some evacuees are still in their hosts' communities, rebuilding the life that was lost in the flood.

MoveOn.org started in 1998, the product of two software entrepreneurs frustrated with the gridlock in Washington. The theory was simple: using the Internet, bring real people to the table in American politics, and hold leaders accountable to them. Our online organization started around a common-sense appeal: to stop the Clinton impeachment that was distracting from the business of the nation, censure him and Move On.

The organization grew by word of mouth as Wes and Joan's email was passed through networks of colleagues and friends. After two months, almost half a million Americans had signed on. And in the seven years since then, we've grown to serve over three million people across the United States.

Most of our members haven't been politically involved before; they wouldn't call themselves activists. But they love this country and they share a determination to lift it up. On the MoveOn staff, we believe our job is to serve the—to identify the ways they can have a voice and a say.

Until HurricaneHousing, this mostly meant weighing in on legislation. MoveOn members wrote heartfelt letters to their members of Congress about campaign finance reform; they held candles at vigils across the land to mark the losses of war; they called their representatives' offices to argue for media reform. In battles large and small, they provided a popular counterweight to lobbyist-driven big money politics.

But in the face of the national calamity of Katrina, they went further than they'd gone before. In the past, they'd given their time and sometimes, their money. After Katrina, they opened up their homes and their lives.

Of course, it wasn't just MoveOn members. From across the political spectrum, others joined them. Some of the emails that moved me most were from people who wrote disclaimers in their postings on the website, noting that they couldn't stand our politics but they shared our inclination to help those who were struggling.

If Hurricane Katrina showed nature in its wildest form, it also showed that a nation divided could come together to take care of people tossed to the wind. And if at the heart of democracy is the idea that we're all responsible for each other, it showed that democracy is deeply alive in American hearts.

Hurricane Katrina produced many tears, but this book isn't just about them. This book is about remembering what endured. It's about the courage and generosity of taking in a stranger in need. It's about the bonds forged in the heat of disaster. And it's about remembering that in the face of an act of God, Americans gave a biblical response: "Love thy neighbor." ⇨

Cots set up for Hurricane Katrina evacuees at the Reliant Center in Houston, TX.

INTRODUCTION

Laura Dawn, Cultural Director, MoveOn.org

I've worked with MoveOn.org for about two-and-a-half years now. I've never had any particular sympathy with political parties – in fact, I personally think the country would be much better off without them. But I believe strongly in the power of MoveOn.org and the growing movement to keep our elected officials accountable and in touch with the needs of everyday Americans.

I've been lucky enough to work on many great projects with MoveOn.org, but I've never felt more honored than while working on HurricaneHousing.org and on this book. Watching HurricaneHousing move from idea to fruition in about two days was truly like witnessing the formation of hope. And reading the listings as they came in, each one an offer of shelter and safety, felt like being in the presence of a miracle. Being able to be part of that effort was simply a blessing I will never forget.

During the aftermath of Hurricane Katrina, millions of Americans (myself included) could not tear themselves away from the televised spectacle of thousands of evacuees clearly in constant danger. The national infrastructure that we thought solid had failed and many of us struggled with a kind of desperate collective guilt.

When faced with the shameful images of people in our own country left to suffer and possibly die, what else can we cling to but the simple hope that our small collective efforts can make a difference?

It's easy to be discouraged. It's easy to fear that our donations of money, time or space are just a drop in a vast insur-mountable bucket. We need desperately to at least hope that our giving is meaningful.

I see no greater evidence of this than in the stories contained in this book.

One of the integral parts of Hurricane Housing.org was getting the 800 number up and running. Obviously, many evacuees wouldn't have access to the Internet, so the 800 number was key. But it also had an unintended effect. Each day, the operators would report, many times in tears, that the evacuees would frequently just talk to them. After receiving the necessary numbers and information, they would stay on the phone and just talk. And their stories were heartbreaking—full of details that no one saw on their TV screens. Their stories were full of courage and hardship; their stories begged for the kind of understanding that only arises from one human being sharing their experience with another. They clearly needed to talk and our 800 operators ended up listening.

The evacuees were also calling the operators back to report something else: the incredible miracle that awaited so many of them at their new homes with their host families. They reported communities banding together to help literally save their lives. They reported that these virtual strangers who took them in during their time of need—across cultural and socio-economic lines, regardless of color or religion—were becoming their *family*.

When I heard this, I knew that we had to somehow document these stories. I immediately hunted down a photographer and an interviewer who were ready to hit the road. From September 23rd to October 6th, 2005, photographer C. B. Smith and interviewer Mark Huntley traveled the country in a rental car, staying in the cheapest possible hotels and interviewing up to five families a day. From my home office in Brooklyn, my good friend Bernardo Issel and I worked every day to keep them moving, searching through listings and finding participating families who wanted to tell their stories.

I have always been a big fan of Studs Terkel's *Working* and its 2000 homage by Word.com, *Gig: Americans Talk About Their Jobs*. Both books relied on extensive interviews, but were edited into first-person narratives that let readers experience the interviewees' tales in a more direct fashion.

I edited *It Takes A Nation* with this in mind, trying to let each person's voice, vernacular and story ring through. For two weeks in December, a small editing team (Sabin Streeter, Pete Nelson, Annie Nocenti and Daron Murphy) and I edited and re-interviewed and re-edited around the clock. I shaped the final book for another two weeks, and by January 10th, 2006, *It Takes a Nation* was born. With an eye on getting this out as soon as possible to continue to raise funds and awareness for the evacuees, the project was taken from conception to finish in about three months. I've presented their interviews without commentary. As you'll see from reading this book, Americans, especially those reared in the great oral traditions of the South, have no problem speaking very clearly for themselves.

C. B. Smith's photographs are a revelation. These are not simply portraits of those involved in HurricaneHousing.org; they reveal a new paradigm of the American family and community. They are beautiful pictures of how and where we live, full of the individualism and spirit that we can define as uniquely American.

Imagine, for a moment, that your home and everything in it has been destroyed. Imagine that you have nothing but the clothes on your back. Imagine that this has simultaneously happened to your entire extended family. Where would you go? What would you do?

The survivors of Hurricane Katrina and the good folks who helped them have something to say. In these stories, we can see that bonds have been forged, barriers have been broken down, and hearts have been opened in a way that just might save us all.

Please listen, and let yourself hope. ⇨

From: Noah T. Winer, MoveOn.org Civic Action
Date: Thursday, September 1, 2005
Subject: Emergency housing drive at
www.hurricanehousing.org. Pass it on.

Dear MoveOn member,

Hurricane Katrina's toll on communities, homes and lives has devastated the nation. Now victims must face the daunting question of where to go next—and we can help. Tens of thousands of newly homeless families are being bused to a stadium in Houston, where they may wait for weeks or months. At least 80,000 are competing for area shelters, and countless more are in motels, cars, or wherever they can stay out of the elements. The Federal Emergency Management Agency and the Red Cross are scrambling to find shelter for the displaced.

This morning, we've launched an emergency national housing drive to connect your empty beds with hurricane victims who desperately need a place to wait out the storm. You can post your offer of housing (a spare room, extra bed, even a decent couch) and search for available housing online at:

www.hurricanehousing.org

Housing is most urgently needed within reasonable driving distance (about 300 miles) of the affected areas in the Southeast, especially New Orleans.

Please forward this message to anyone you know in the region who might be able to help.

But no matter where you live, your housing could still make a world of difference to a person or family in need, so please offer what you can.

The process is simple:

* You can sign up to become a host by posting a description of whatever housing you have available, along with contact information. You can change or remove your offer at any time.
* Hurricane victims, local and national relief organizations, friends and relatives can search the site for housing. We'll do everything we can to get your offers where they are needed most. Many shelters actually already have Internet access, but folks without Net access can still make use of the site through caseworkers and family members.
* Hurricane victims or relief agencies will contact hosts and together decide if it's a good match and make the necessary travel arrangements.

The host's address is not released until a particular match is agreed on.

If hosting doesn't work for you, please consider donating to the Red Cross to help with the enormous tasks of rescue and recovery. You can give online at:

www.moveon.org

As progressives, we share a core belief that we are all in this together, and today is an important chance to put that idea to work. There are thousands of families who have just lost everything and need a place to stay dry. Let's do what we can to help.

Thanks for being there when it matters most.

—**Noah T. Winer and the whole MoveOn.org**
Civic Action Team ⇨

In Southern Louisiana, Sea Falcon and Sea Wolf, along with a few smaller sailboats washed up onto this road.

I really hope I can help someone by providing a safe, welcoming home for up to a year. My house is old but completely comfortable and safe. I live in South St. Louis City right across from a very large park. I have a full bedroom to spare with a bathroom to share. I have a nice kitchen and deck to enjoy cooking with guests. I have two dogs that are quite friendly, but I think it would be safest to have any children be over age 12. I'd prefer a female guest but will keep all options open. I would be able to accept two people and one dog for around a year. I will help them look for a job, provide transportation when I can and anything else to make this traumatic transition a little easier and as close to a home as possible. Please accept my offer with open arms and an open heart.

JULIE O.
ST. LOUIS, MISSOURI

> "WE LIVED ON THAT PROPERTY FOR five generations. It's kind of hard to let go of. The dirt gets in your blood ... the sweat and toil that goes into it. We put a lot into that home."

GILDA WILLIAMS: I lived at 3914 Louisa Street in New Orleans. It's a family home, a single-family property, and well, we were comfortable. It was fully furnished with a big living room, kitchen, dining room, three bedrooms, den, a bathroom and a half, wash room, *big* yard. Lots of land. We had fruit trees, all kinds of stuff growin' out there. That property has been in my family for five generations.

My daughter, Lanzelle—now she had her own apartment in New Orleans East. But at one time I had all my kids there at my home on Louisa Street. My grandkids was always running in and out, you know, and my friend Trahon came over from time to time…

So, you know, it was just going well. I was an office manager for two doctors—with an office of eight other doctors that leased from them. You know, admit/discharge, billing—insurance verification in a hospital setting or a medical office setting. Yeah, that's my specialty. I've been doing that for 13 years. I *was* looking for a second income, because, as we all know, Christmas is coming up, and you know, Christmas is important to the grandkids. *Very* important to the grandkids! (*Laughs*)

Anyway. We just didn't expect the storm to do as much damage as it did.

It was Sunday and Trahon was over. We heard that the mayor declared it mandatory for us to leave. So, we thought, OK, we'll have to spend some money on hotels or whatever. But then my daughter called me. Now, I thought she had already gone out of town with her grandmother, my ex-husband's mom. So when she called

it shocked me because I had thought she had gone with my grandkids. I thought I didn't have anybody to worry about: my son had evacuated, his family had gone with him, everybody was safe, or so I thought. And I was even considering staying, just 'cause I thought everyone I loved was safe and you know, I thought, *Y'all just go, I ain't goin' nowhere!* (*Laughs*)

But when my daughter called, well, it kinda kicked me in the you-know-where, and I thought, *Well, maybe we all better get out of here.*

And I remember this so distinctly: I walked over to the sink and I heard the house *creak*. It just went *errrrrrr*. It was a strange sound to me, a sound I hadn't heard my house make before. And right then, I had a vision: in my mind's eye, I saw the water clean up to the ceiling in my house. And I thought, *This has to be a warning.*

You see, Louisa Street is a pass street, and sometimes when a truck will pass, the house will move a little or something. But I never heard it creak like that, like it could give way. So when I heard that, I just thought it was God's way of telling me, "Time to GO." Time to get the heck out of Dodge.

So Trahon got the car ready and Lanzelle came by. Her ex-husband dropped her off. …(*Starts crying*) That was the last time we saw him. He…he's dead. He passed away. We don't know why yet. He had some breathing problems…and he swam through that terrible water. He got caught in that terrible water. (*Juan puts his hand on her arm as she cries.*)

GILDA: (*takes a big breath*) So. Me and Trahon and Lanzelle got into the car, and it took us six hours to go from New Orleans to Brookhaven, Mississippi, where our friends John and Sylvia live. Which is usually a forty-five minute drive. It's only 150 miles. You hit 70 and…you know (*laughing*) don't tell anybody that I…that I speed like that! But you hit 70 and 45 minutes, later you're there. But not

[left to right] Juan Salinas (host), Gilda Williams (evacuee), Trahon (evacuee)

that day. And you know what was cute? A lot of the Mississippi residents were standing on the bridges that cross the interstate highway, waving banners that said "God Bless You" and wishing us well. It was such a positive thing.

When we got to John and Sylvia's, the storm was hitting there too—hit so hard that a tree fell on their house and knocked the power out. We were all there living together for about five days without power. And we were not the only people Sylvia and John were putting up. There were about twenty-two of us total staying at their house, in the dark with no access to news or nothing.

We were all just trying to make the best of it. People's nerves were frazzled and stuff. It was a hard living situation.

So it was stormin' and rainin' and we noticed that all the men kept going out to the car. I'm thinkin', "What you all goin' to the car for?" (*Laughs*) I'm nosy! So I go up there. Well, it turns out one of the men in the group had a television that he could plug into the car lighter and they're lookin' at the news about New Orleans. And I'm like, "Well, what are they sayin'? What are they sayin'?"

Well, they're saying on the news that we can't go back. Maybe ever.

They didn't have many pictures of New Orleans at that time because we were getting a lot of news about Mississippi. We were in Mississippi, so, you know, that's what you get: Mississippi news.

On the fourth day, the policemen in Brookhaven were goin' house to house makin' sure everybody was fine. And I asked them, "When can we go back to New Orleans?" That's what happens after the hurricane, right? You can go back home. But this time…

The policeman, he just looked at me and his face got white, white, white. He says, (*her voice chokes up*): "You can't go back home. There's bodies floatin' everywhere."

I couldn't…I couldn't believe it.

So we had to decide what to do next. I told Trahon I wanted to come to Chicago—my son lives here and I hadn't seen him in a while, so, you know, let's go to Chicago. And maybe New Orleans will open back up.

So we hit the road and we drove all those hours. … We were so tired. Trahon got us here. I'm no good at driving. I get behind the wheel of a car and just want to drive right to the rest stop and get some sleep! No, Trahon got us here, he really did.

Now, we wanted to go to my son's, but I didn't have my address book, no phone numbers, nothin'. But I remembered that he worked at the Ramada Inn. So we just came into town, asked where the Ramada Inn was, got directions and found our way to it and that's when we met with my son. He has a small apartment and a roommate, so we were really putting him out. But they were so good to us. We stayed with them for a few nights, but we obviously couldn't stay there for very long because it was just too small and crowded. So Trahon went to the Evacuee Resource Center.

JUAN SALINAS: The intake center for Chicago.

GILDA: Right. And they gave him Juan's number to contact, which they had from the HurricaneHousing site, and they spoke over the phone. Juan came over in person and brought Trahon to see the house. I was applying for a job at the time.

JUAN: I live in Countryside, Illinois, about a half hour west of Chicago. I'm an investor. I own property and I buy real estate in Chicago that I rent out. And when everything happened in New Orleans, I happened to have this place vacant. So I went on the Internet and posted it on HurricaneHousing.org. I saw something on the TV about the website, so that's the one I went to. And about a week after I posted, I heard from Trahon. I had several calls about it, before and after, but they were either looking for a different location or they had too many people.

I wouldn't say it was "natural" for me to post my property online. I did think about it a little bit. But not like, should I or shouldn't I? I mean, it wasn't that difficult. It was the right thing to do. I had something available and since it was empty, somebody could use it, you know? It wasn't a hard decision.

The website was easy to use. Fill it out, fill in the blanks, that kind of thing. So anyway, Trahon called me and they weren't real familiar with the city, but their son lived fairly close by, so that was a point of reference. So Gilda and Trahon came over and saw the place and they liked it and moved in, just like that.

GILDA: And I should tell you, Juan didn't just give us a house. He brought furniture, dishes, even food and cleaning supplies. He didn't just put us here and leave us. He literally took care of us, you know what I'm saying? And his family is beautiful. From his wife Betty to his three little girls. I haven't met his son yet. And his mom-in-law. I mean, these are really wonderful people. We were blessed, blessed to be taken in and blessed to be bonded with him.

Oh yes. He helped us out tremendously. And of course, he's not gonna say anything but I'm gonna say it!

JUAN: *(Laughs)*

GILDA: I'm gonna say it out loud because he has a big heart and his family has a big heart. And you don't always find that. But I've found that ever since we've been in communication with this man...I'd think about stuff, I'm telling you, I'm not kidding, I'd say, what else do we need? And I'd start to make a list and he wouldn't be anywhere around but all a sudden he'd pop up at the door with the same stuff I had on my list! And I'm like, oh my God, this man has telepathy.

JUAN: *(Laughs)*

GILDA: So we're like family now. We had him over for dinner and cooked some red beans.

JUAN: New Orleans stuff!

GILDA: We had red beans and rice, and some fried chicken, lots of fresh fruit. We had a good time.

JUAN: What was that cabbage you made the other day, the smothered cabbage? That was a different kind of cabbage!

GILDA: Oh yeah, he's used to white cabbage. This was white cabbage and green cabbage combined. What we do is smother it with lots of spices and serve it with rice and corn—it's like a stewed cabbage.

So we have a home here. But it's been a bit of a transition. The climate so far is a lot like ours. They warned me though about the winter. And they brought me blankets and clothes and stuff, and let me know what to expect as far as cold is concerned.

I am actively seeking employment. My daughter has a position that's been offered to her, thank God, in security at the Chicago University Hospital. But of course, with her children's father passing...well, it will delay her start date. But she wants that job. She needs that job. And I need one too. And...well, this is a big, big city. Just learning how to get around... Juan, I should tell you. I got lost again, Juan.

JUAN: Again?? *(Laughter)*

GILDA: I got lost three times in this city! Just trying to get my bearings. It's just much, much bigger than New Orleans. I could go from one end of New Orleans to the other end in, say, twenty-five minutes. Here, it takes hours! And people...millions of people. My God, it's a lot of people here.

JUAN: Can we talk about FEMA for a second? Because the city has done some things for evacuees and FEMA has done some stuff. ...

GILDA: Okay, um, I applied for FEMA online. And they submitted me the first payment, which has helped me to more or less get settled and get a lot of things that I didn't get through donations, and that was good. It made me feel like, at least okay, I got some stability, you know. I also applied for unemployment insurance, through Louisiana, but I haven't received it yet. And here in Chicago, the city has a program of emergency funds for transients or displaced people and they gave us what they call a Link card to buy food with. And that was good. But other than the food card and the money from FEMA—well, that's it. I mean, we don't have anything else. We have nothing else.

Just kindnesses. But you don't want to wear out kindnesses, and hurt someone else in the process.

JUAN: Right now, we're actually trying to work out a more permanent arrangement and I really hope that works out.

GILDA: Me too. I don't know if it's possible to return to New Orleans. My daughter, after all this happening with my son-in-law...she's feelin' she never wants to see New Orleans again. I need to be here with her for a good portion of this time to help her through, get her straight, get her settled. But I'll be visiting down there soon to handle business because I was told that I had to meet with FEMA on our family property.

JUAN: Five generations or so on that home, right?

GILDA: Yeah. Five generations. We lived on that property for five generations.

So you know...it's kind of hard to let go of. The dirt gets in your blood. The sweat and toil that goes into it, I mean...we put a lot into that home.

But from what I understand it's underwater.

I have not seen it. I have not seen it. A police officer friend of mine said, "Don't go back, you don't want to see it." He said, "It's going to break your heart." But I don't know if he's just saying that to me to keep me from going back and getting my little heart broken, or if he's actually seen it. I'm not sure. (*Long pause*)

But I will tell you...and this is from the heart...I really feel betrayed. By the local government and the state government. I don't believe that they actually stressed the importance of shoring up those levees. I used to follow the City Council meetings and things of that nature on television. And I would watch as each representative would go to the local government and ask 'em: "Okay, we need x amount of dollars to shore up the levee system." And time after time, they were denied. I saw the Corps of Engineers tell them, "We've run out of money, we can't finish this project that we started at South Claiborne Avenue and Napoleon." That's where all those dead bodies were found at that hospital. It used to be called Southern Baptist but it's Memorial Medical Center now. When they start construction they don't complete, they leave you vulnerable. And that is what I believe actually happened to the City of New Orleans.

And on the federal level—I have to feel as if they should have come sooner. They should have come before the storm. We have military sites all over. There's one on the West Bank, there's one on the East Bank, on the Lakefront. They moved all of the military trucks out...and those trucks were all empty. They could have taken people out in those trucks, for the same amount of gas, and saved lives. But it wasn't important to them.

Yeah, I'm angry. I'm very angry with them all. Because the storm didn't hit us. The storm veered to the right of us. We were on what they call the good side of the storm. Less winds on the right side and we were on the right side.

The storm was not what devastated our city. No, it was man. It was man that let those levees break and man who didn't get us out in time.

JUAN: Well, I just wanna say that helping these folks has been rewarding...something I am fortunate to be a part of, you know? It feels good to me to have been able to help them.

People gotta realize when someone needs a hand and you're able to do it, why not? Look—whenever we go, whenever we die—none of this is going with you. Gilda and I were talking the other day about how on the same spot we're standing right now, hundreds of people have stood here before, and they don't take it with them when they die. It's still here—this land, the world, you know? Long after we're gone. We just stand here for a short while. Someone else is gonna be here a hundred years from now, doing something else, and they won't even know we were here. So...do the good that you can do now. That's all I'm saying. And I hope Gilda can get her home back eventually. And I hope we can come down and visit!

GILDA: Oh, definitely. We want him to come down so bad. (*Laughs*) Once we're up and running we want him and his whole family to come down. Yep. Come down and spend some time with us so we can extend... .

JUAN: Some more good cooking? (*Laughs*) 'Cause, see, that's the whole payoff! I did it all for her food. I don't wanna lie, I love her food! (*Laughter*)

GILDA: One more thing before we're through. I need to get my grandkids up here. And I'm just not connecting with the right federal department. I called Red Cross, I called the FEMA back, I called the Habitat line, you know. They are in Rain, Louisiana with my ex-mother-in-law and their great-grandmother. It's three kids, two girls and a boy: Zaide Tian Cayette, Christina Ascenscia Cayette and Enrique Antonio Cayette. Yeah, that's my daughter's children!

We need to get them up here because my daughter has taken a blow with their daddy dying and they all need to be together. We have just enough money to drive down to the funeral. But getting back is gonna be an issue. I did call an additional disaster line for Red Cross and the lady's supposed to be calling me back. She put my name on the reunification list, they call it.

It's a lot of paperwork, all of it. You gotta be organized. You know (*smiles and gestures at interviewer*), like you and your little notebook. I got one too. ➪

Church steeple toppled by high winds.

"**I SAID TO MYSELF, 'I HAVE GOT TO DO** something.' I said, 'What's the worst that can happen if I took someone in?' Okay. I came up with a couple scenarios. *(Laughs)* But I'm a MoveOn supporter. I was thinking that I would love to help somebody. And I just did it. The HurricaneHousing email came and I said, 'I've got to do it.'"

OFORI ATTA DANQUAH: I'm from Ghana, West Africa. That's my roots. I'd been living in New Orleans for five years, on my own, in my own apartment. I was a Xavier University college student. Chemistry major. I was a manager at a Rite Aid there and was also delivering pizza for extra money. When we heard that a storm was coming, we had about a week to leave the city. I had no choice.

Fortunately and unfortunately, my fiancée Sophia, who is also originally from Ghana, had come all the way from Japan for a visit. She had been in New Orleans going on three weeks and we were having a good time. So when the storm hit, my fiancée was also in New Orleans. And she was so scared. She kept saying, "Let's go. Let's go." But where are we going?

I had a friend in Chicago; that was four or five years back. He's from Cameroon, West Africa. He's the only guy I know that lives elsewhere in the United States. I was trying to get in touch with him because we had only two more days to leave the city. He wasn't responding. Honestly, I didn't even know if he was still in Chicago, but I had nowhere else to go.

So at the eleventh hour, I called this friend of mine at Xavier, who was driving to Michigan. I told him, "My fiancée and I will ride with you. Drop us somewhere in Chicago. Is it okay?" He says, "Why not?" So I went to him

with only two clothes, because I thought I was going to be gone for only two days. We just took off. When we finally got to Chicago, he left us somewhere in Cottage Grove and said, "Ofori, this is your final destination. I've got to go up to Michigan."

And here I am in a whole huge city, with my fiancée, and we have nowhere to go.

We were wandering around. We didn't have enough money on us, and had to save the little we had for contingency purposes. It was getting late in the night and we needed to find someplace to stay. So we went into the emergency ward of a hospital and we pretended that we are patients. *(Laughs)* Yeah.

There were a lot of people sitting on chairs waiting to be called. They had a roof over their head, you know. So we pretend we are also waiting for a doctor. We can sit there as long as we can. People were sleeping so we got us some sleep. We spent two days there, with no questions. During the day, we just stepped out. Evening time, we just come back again.

Then I got a text message from...well, I don't know who it was from. It was this 800 number to call for help. I called and this lady was more than willing to help me. Actually, it's amazing. I don't know if it was something with Xavier University? Trying to help their students? Anyway, I told them that I was in Chicago and they gave me a direct number. It was the Red Cross.

I go to the Red Cross; I tell them my story. I think I was the only one who had nowhere to go, the only one who didn't know anybody in the city. So I was given special treatment. A volunteer offered us a place to sleep. But they had cats in their house, and my fiancée is allergic to cats. So we had to decline that offer. And then this lady from Xavier said, "You can sleep on my friend's couch until they find you a place where you'll be comfortable."

This was where I met Ronnie at the Red Cross. And Ronnie said, "I'm going to go on the Internet. There are

[left to right] Marilyn Eisenberg (host), Ofori Atta Danquah (evacuee)

more people willing to help. So you go spend the night somewhere, and I'll get back with you very soon."

RONNIE WALKER: I am a clinical counselor and I've been a Red Cross volunteer for five years. I had just gotten the email from MoveOn.org about hurricane housing. I checked it out. The first name on the list for Chicago was Marilyn Eisenberg. I gave her a call and I said, "Um…you don't know me." (Laughs) "We're looking for housing. There's a lovely gentleman and his fiancée…" I think we talked for maybe five minutes. And Marilyn said, "Okay, I'll come right down."

I didn't know her before, but Marilyn lives in the same neighborhood I do. I've been there forever, for thirty-four years. It's a real community. We all just called up different people and said, "We've got these two evacuees. They need clothes." And we just walked up and down our block to get them what they needed.

Because talking to FEMA was like talking to a black hole. It's like sailing a paper airplane into the Grand Canyon. We came up with a new term, PSFD: Post-Traumatic FEMA Disorder. Much of the trauma people had was from trying to deal with FEMA.

As I mentioned, I am a clinical counselor. The Red Cross uses counselors, so I often get called in for disasters. The third day after the hurricane, I got a call from them, "Can you come down to the phone banks?" They were getting 1,500 to 2,000 calls a day, and they wanted some mental health counselors there. We were getting calls like, "I can't find my husband," "I'd like to volunteer," "Who's taking care of the animals?" "I'm stranded on the road." That kind of thing.

United Airlines had an empty plane and they'd flown supplies in to New Orleans. So they filled the return flight with 104 evacuees. This was before the National Guard was even in there. These people had been in the water for three days. So I was working with evacuees literally fresh out of the water and they had literally flooded into Chicago. They sent four or five of us down to the O'Hare airport to greet them, and I worked with them for about two weeks. We were in the red carpet lounge and—I've got to give this to United—they kept the press far away, to give these people their privacy. When those evacuees came off the plane, they were numb, so traumatized. They just walked in single-file, numb. The first thing that hit me was the stench, the stench of the water. You see, they hadn't changed their clothes and they had all been in that water for three days. I've never seen people look like that. … (starts to cry)

People were missing teeth. One woman was missing her dentures. They had just run for their lives, without grabbing anything. They didn't have ID or their phone books. Some were disabled or mentally ill.

United had stacks of clean T-shirts. We realized there were no pants, so we ran down to the Lost and Found and got pants for people. United had hot roast beef sandwiches and they had arranged with a nearby Hilton Hotel for free showers for them. United was willing to fly them anywhere. United was great and they didn't use this as a press moment. They gave people their dignity.

So you know, FEMA was not working, and it took a whole community to help these people.

MARILYN EISENBERG: I had been watching what was going on, especially in the Superdome. I said to myself, "I have got to do something". I said, "What's the worst that can happen if I took someone in?" Okay. I came up with a couple scenarios. (Laughs) But I'm a MoveOn supporter. I was thinking that I would love to help somebody. And I just did it. The Hurricane Housing email came and I said, "I've got to do it".

OFORI: Imagine walking on the streets, having nothing in mind. Where am I going to sleep? Sleeping in the hospital waiting room. Thinking about how my stuff is gone for good. Stuff that I've taken five years to build. It's gone. And then all of a sudden, living in a very luxurious home. Through people who are more than willing to accept me. I couldn't know how to put that into words. Because when we moved in here, Marilyn said, "You know what? This is your home. Do whatever you want to do here. This is your key. Come move in and come in at any time you want."

It was just too much for me. I was still going through a lot, and what she told me was: "You've got to get control of your life. I'm going to put you back into school. Because you were a student at Xavier and that's the only way you can get control of your life." The next thing, she put me in a car. "Go get yourself registered. Make sure you are in school." She drove me to UIC.

MARILYN: UIC, University of Illinois at Chicago, is a huge campus. It's synonymous to NYU. They have a marvelous pharmacy school here and Ofori wants to be a pharmacist.

OFORI: It's like, wherever I needed to go, she was willing to take me. Go to school. Get registered. And I went there. Did what was asked of me. Got myself enrolled.

Actually, if I could get into school, I figured they would give me a place to sleep. That's all I wanted: to work hard and study late hours and to have a safe place to sleep. So I went into the college and spoke to the counselor, who told me that I could be counted as an out-of-state student. And the very next day I was in school.

Sophia, my fiancée, was supposed to be leaving by the close of September. And I figured we should cut her vacation short, because this is not a vacation anymore. So please, just go early, I told her. You have a job in Japan. Start doing something. Till I get on my feet, then you can come back and have a very nice vacation with me. And she understood.

MARILYN: But she was here for, oh, two weeks. That Tuesday when Ofori started UIC, Sophia and I got dressed. I said, "C'mon, we'll go down and volunteer at the Salvation Army." And so we did that. She volunteered every day after that. She put in eight to ten hours a day. So it was all about getting control of your life.

Sophia was just amazing. Here she is, all the way from Japan, getting caught up in all this. She kept saying, "You saved our lives." I told her what I always say: "Go from being part of the problem to being part of the solution." She volunteered at the Salvation Army and she just blossomed.

OFORI: Marilyn came to pick me up from school the other day, because we were going to see if I could get food stamps. We had to go through some process. When she came, she said, "Guess what I have for you? You're going to be happy. I have an apartment for you, rent-free, for three months. And it's not just one single-room apartment. It's a three-bedroom apartment!" (*Laughs*)

MARILYN: They could stay there starting that night. I'm serious. Absolutely. Totally. And this apartment is right in the university area, in Little Italy. It's right by UIC.

OFORI: It's walking distance. Yeah. It's awesome.

MARILYN: I happen to be involved on the board of the Children's Museum, and the Children's Museum had put out an email saying, "We are going to offer temporary jobs to anyone affected from Children's Museums in the Gulf." So I called the person that was heading it up, and I said, "I have someone here and he's not with the Children's Museum, but I'd like to have you interview him for a job." So Ofori went down and interviewed, and now he's working at the Children's Museum.

OFORI: Front desk. I'm working with the computer. Taking money from parents and allowing the children to go in and have fun. And I have another job waiting for me, at Walgreens. When Ronnie took me to her neighborhood, everybody came together trying to help. There was this doctor. He said, "I'm going to talk directly to the Walgreens district office and make sure that there is a vacancy somewhere." I really want this job because it relates to my academic work as a pharmaceutical technician. When I got home, I got a call, and there's this lady at the district office that I have to go see for an interview.

I filled out an application. I have to do the drug test. And this lady told me that since I came from New Orleans, they need to do a background check. That's going to take a few weeks. But that's the only thing I'm waiting on and if everything comes through right, I'll get to start working right away. So I'll be working two jobs. Money! And school! Actually, my background check is going to be very difficult, because Xavier is closed down. The Museum, I don't know how they did it, because they also went online checking on my background. They came up with something good. (*Laughs*)

MARILYN: Now we'll see him get through a winter in Chicago. Because they think they want to settle here, but we'll see. (*Laughs*) I'm not putting my chips on that table yet.

OFORI: Well, you know, everything I had is gone. I don't know what specifically happened, but I know that the parish all got flooded. My building was eight feet underwater, so you can imagine... And Chicago is a nice place to live.

RONNIE: He knows he has family here.

OFORI: I have lovely family here.

MARILYN: All of us. (*Laughter*)

OFORI: All of you. Everybody. So far it is awesome. Positive. But if I can go back to the reminiscing…If I have to spend one dollar on something, it means I love it. I cherish it. What I spent all my money on before—my furniture, my clothes, my belongings in New Orleans—it's all gone. I have family pictures. I have my documents. Apart from that, I don't have anything.

But any time I tend to think about that, I have some shoulders to cry on. Marilyn will talk to me. She'll say, "Where you are in this new life? Things will get better. Stay positive. You know, let it go. Every misfortune is a blessing."

I mean, it's so nice to meet nice people that are more than willing to help. So I think I'll take this opportunity to say thank you to all of them.

You in America have the pros and cons. You have the positive side and some of the negative side, too. I was one time eating at a restaurant somewhere here in Chicago. I think on Rice Street? People were watching CNN about the hurricane. People were drinking, sharing their views. I was eating, but I was also paying attention to the people around me. People said, "Why would they stay there till this hurricane comes to meet them? This is sheer stupidity. These people are stupid. They should have gone. They should have left the city."

And I prayed for one second. I asked my Lord to give them a little understanding, to give them the wisdom to understand what is actually going on. Because I was a victim. I didn't have nowhere to go. The people of New Orleans, they had nowhere to go. They were praying; they were hoping this thing doesn't come to New Orleans. Because if they had to leave New Orleans, they had no way to do it.

The people in the bar were very callous, very, very callous. And I said to them, "You know what? Maybe the people in New Orleans don't have the means to leave the city. They don't have the means of transportation. They have nowhere to go. Like me."

So why would they talk about these people like this? I would think they would feel sympathy for them.

MARILYN: Actually, the realization that I've come to is that, what if we all went out and did this with one homeless person on the street? We could end homelessness tomorrow. Now that's a different customer, so to speak. There are mentally ill people out there that can't possibly do what Ofori and Sophia did. They can't in a matter of days take control of their lives and move on and get their lives organized. But what if? So that's what I've been thinking about a lot. What if. And would I ever have the guts to take in a homeless person?

Ofori, should I share the letter you sent me?

OFORI: Sure. My goodness. You can. You can do it. Because you know, it takes courage for you to put your name on the Internet and say, "I have a room I'm going to offer a stranger." Somebody you don't know. You don't know his background. You don't know him or her. It could be a maniac. Could be an armed robber. Could be a drug addict. Could be…

MARILYN: But it was you. (reading Ofori's letter): *When I took off from New Orleans, I had no knowledge of where I was going to stay. But I had to run for my life. In Chicago our best choice was to wander around with little or no hope. Then out of the blue you came to my rescue when I needed one. You gave us food, clothes, and sheltered us without asking for a dime. All your phone calls were centered around us. Your strong words of encouragement lifted my spirit when I was virtually down. You provided a shoulder to be cried on. Yes, you are an angel. Your benevolence is highly recognized in heaven. The words "thank you" hardly seem enough, but they're coming from my heart. A heart uplifted by your kindness. Please accept my gratitude for everything that you've done.*

See, it could have been anyone. But it was you, Ofori. It was you. ⇨

The town water tower in Buras, LA on top of a house.

> "I PLAY BARITONE SAXOPHONE AND tenor saxophone, and then I sing. The horn parts I play are somewhat abrasive in certain songs—kind of angry—almost as if you're celebrating the last day on Earth."

JOSH COHEN: I was a self-employed musician and glass blower in New Orleans. My bread and butter way of making a living was the glass blowing. I did commission and consignment work for different shops and galleries and stuff. I was doing it at a studio that's accessible to the public for rental. So I would rent time—actually paying by the hour—to get my product done. At that kind of place, if you don't execute your project well—tough luck. You still have to pay. It's like having to pay to go to work instead of *getting paid* to work. So it's kind of a gamble. But if you're good, it's a decent way to make a living.

I was also in a band—still am actually, I guess—called the Morning 40 Federation, which was a blast. We were sort of a New Orleans institution, together about seven or eight years. We play very New Orleans-style, celebrational rock music. Our name for the sound is "drunk rock." (*Laughs*) Now, obviously, you can't put music into words. But if I had to describe it, I would say that it's like rock, but kinda horn-driven. I play baritone saxophone and tenor saxophone, and then I sing. The horn parts I play are somewhat abrasive in certain songs—kind of angry—almost as if you're celebrating the last day on Earth. All in all, our music is real raucous kinda stuff.

So that was me: blowin' glass and playin' in a crazy drunk rock band, just kinda doing my thing. Then we got the storm. And, well, at first I didn't think much of it. In fact, I was gonna stay and ride the whole thing out. I had a kinda stubborn, hold-down-the-fort mentality at first.

Then I saw what the hurricane was doin' on TV. And the mayor announced a mandatory evacuation. So my girlfriend said that we better get out of there. She actually went as far as to say, "I'm gonna leave without you if you don't come with me." And then a couple of our friends called and just started yelling and screaming at us to get out. So I gave in. We left. But it was later, you know? Like, Sunday, around 4 or 5 p.m. That was after the hurricane had already been doin' its thing for quite some time.

So we needed to get out of there fast. But the bad thing was we couldn't find gas. We went to about eight different gas stations in New Orleans and none of 'em had anything. We finally found one station with a line of cars all fillin' up. So we waited on that line for about a half hour. And then the moment our turn came—at the very instant we were pickin' up the nozzle and about to put some gas in our tank—they closed the place down! Some dude just grabbed the pump outta my hand and said, "Sorry, no more gas."

So we kept driving around. And we finally found this little place on Esplanade and Claiborne, a real old-school gas station. And because of the way they had it set up—there was no real efficient way to go in there and pay with a credit card—you had to wait in a crazy long line, like twice the size of the line at the place we'd just been. And that's really the reason they still had gas, 'cause it was so hard to actually just buy it and get out of there. Anyway, we waited behind what must have been about twenty cars'. And finally we got our gas and got out of there.

My girlfriend's car is a 1962 Dodge Lancer. It's basically an antique. We wouldn't even usually feel comfortable driving it around to the grocery store because it's so old. And this was the car we're usin' to try and escape, like, one of the worst hurricanes in history. So we just took it real slow and babied the car. We made our way north, just staying in motels or hotels along the way whenever it was time to take a break.

[left to right] Joshua Cohen (evacuee), Brian Enck (host)

At the time, we really weren't sure where we were even headed. At first we were gonna go to D.C., 'cause we had family there. But then I figured, all right, we've got the Adirondack Mountains to consider. With this antique car we were drivin', we really had to decide to go either on the left side of the mountains or the right side. We were very worried about the transmission falling out if we tried to make the climb straight over. So, in order to go on the right side of the mountains, we'd have to head all the way back down to Atlanta and then cut over. If we headed in the other direction, we'd be going towards Ohio, where I was pretty sure I might be able to get a job. So that's what we did.

My friend here in Columbus, Dan Schriber, has a glass studio. And Dan had told me, a while before the hurricane hit, that he'd gotten this big order from a friend of his in England. He had about a thousand Christmas ornaments to make before the holidays and he was lookin' for help. So I thought I could come here and sweat it out in the studio with him for a while. And I've been doin' that ever since I got here. I'm making Christmas balls—just slammin' 'em out—makin' sure the Brits are gonna have a merry Yuletide.

So really, what brought us here to Ohio were Christmas balls! *(Laughs)* And the car, well, that had a lot to do with it as well.

But once we got here, it felt like the right decision. The only problem was we had no decent place to stay. First we tried a combination of crappy hotels. And then we actually tried sleeping on the floor of the dusty glass studio. But my girlfriend wasn't really into the whole bachelor, art studio kind of lifestyle. *(Laughs)* And then my mom told me about this MoveOn.org. And I looked it up on the Internet and got a phone number. I called someone and they actually read the ads over the phone to me. Someone at that MoveOn.org 800 number just walked me through it and even called Brian for me while I waited on the other line. That's how we got connected.

BRIAN ENCK: I live here in Columbus, north of the Ohio State University campus. I didn't know about MoveOn before the hurricane. I think there were three organiza-

tions that I signed up with and MoveOn was the only one that called me back. I just felt like there were people who needed help. And opening up my home seemed like a practical way to lend a hand. It honestly seemed like a no-brainer to me. I have the space. My house is about 1,200 square feet and there are two bedrooms. So I had a spare bedroom and bathroom. And now Josh and his girlfriend are usin' 'em.

JOSH: It's great. Being here has been very comfortable. I thought it might be a little awkward, but we have compatible interests. And it's kinda uncanny—Brian's place is like a parallel universe to my old reality in some ways. Like, his door, you have to kinda slam it. Same with my door back home in New Orleans. You have to give it an extra slam because it's warped. And my TV at home—you can't turn it on or off with the remote control because it makes other electronic things in the house turn on or off as well. It does some weird remote control thing. And Brian's TV has the same problem. One of the first things Brian told me when I got here was, "Just turn the TV on by manually hitting it."

BRIAN: It seems like simple little things, but...

JOSH: I mean, we even had some guy over here drinking beer the other night, just hanging out. And after thinking about it for a second, I realized that he looks exactly like a totally different guy who comes over to my house and drinks beer all the time. Weird Twilight Zone parallels, man! *(Laughs)*

BRIAN: It's reassuring, I guess! *(Laughs)*

JOSH: Oh man. I just feel thankful that we have a nice comfortable home to stay in, with amenities we'd never have at a shelter or someplace like that. I mean, I was even grateful to be able to stay on the floor at my friend's glass studio. But that whole "camping" feeling can get old pretty fast. Here at Brian's place we have cable TV. We can watch Bill Maher, movies. I can watch football. It's just nice to have some luxuries that you take for granted until a catastrophe like this happens. First it was water and gas and hotels and spending a lot of our savings on just basic survival needs and getting my girlfriend's car fixed and stuff like that. And then we fell into the money vortex. We were basically vagabonds on the road, emotionally frazzled, going broke and left without a home. The only reminders of where we used to live were these scary images on CNN. So now it's nice to just have a bed. It's nice to have simple things. Brian's very easy to get along with. And there's a kitchen and a fridge!

BRIAN: Plus we go out drinking.

JOSH: Now that's something I definitely enjoy, ya know? It kinda takes the edge off everything—like work. I mean, normally I wouldn't bc too psyched to spend my life making Christmas balls for hours and hours on end. But I feel humbled by this whole experience. I'm honestly just grateful that I actually have a place to go every day and make a few bucks. And then I get to come back here and hang out with Brian.

I want to go back home to New Orleans. But this is really okay for now. Like, I could sit here and obsess about the fact that they're not allowing the people from my zip code back into New Orleans and that the loading door was blown off of my warehouse, basically giving looters free access to my art studio for the whole time I'm up here. But I'm tryin' not to stress.

And sometimes, it's hard. I mean, my artist studio has just been wide open to the streets for an entire month. And my saxophones are...it's a mystery as to the condition of my saxophones or if they've been stolen. And yesterday, I remembered the fact that we left some deer meat in our freezer. So I can be reasonably positive that at this very moment, a huge hunk of very thawed-out deer meat is spewing maggots in our fridge. It's difficult not to obsess over all that shit. I mean, there are a million ways to go negative. But I've just been trying to catch myself every time I start to slip into that kinda thought pattern and just see the bright side as much as possible.

BRIAN: It's not easy.

JOSH: No, it's not. But as far as net positive, I mean, Brian of course has been a major positive for us. We have a great place to stay. A place where we can just be ourselves and where things seem normal. We can just, like, zone out. 'Cause I feel comfortable around Brian. I feel like I've made a friend.

BRIAN: And I may have a space in New Orleans when I go there to visit.

JOSH: Oh, he's most definitely got a space in New Orleans for life. ⇨

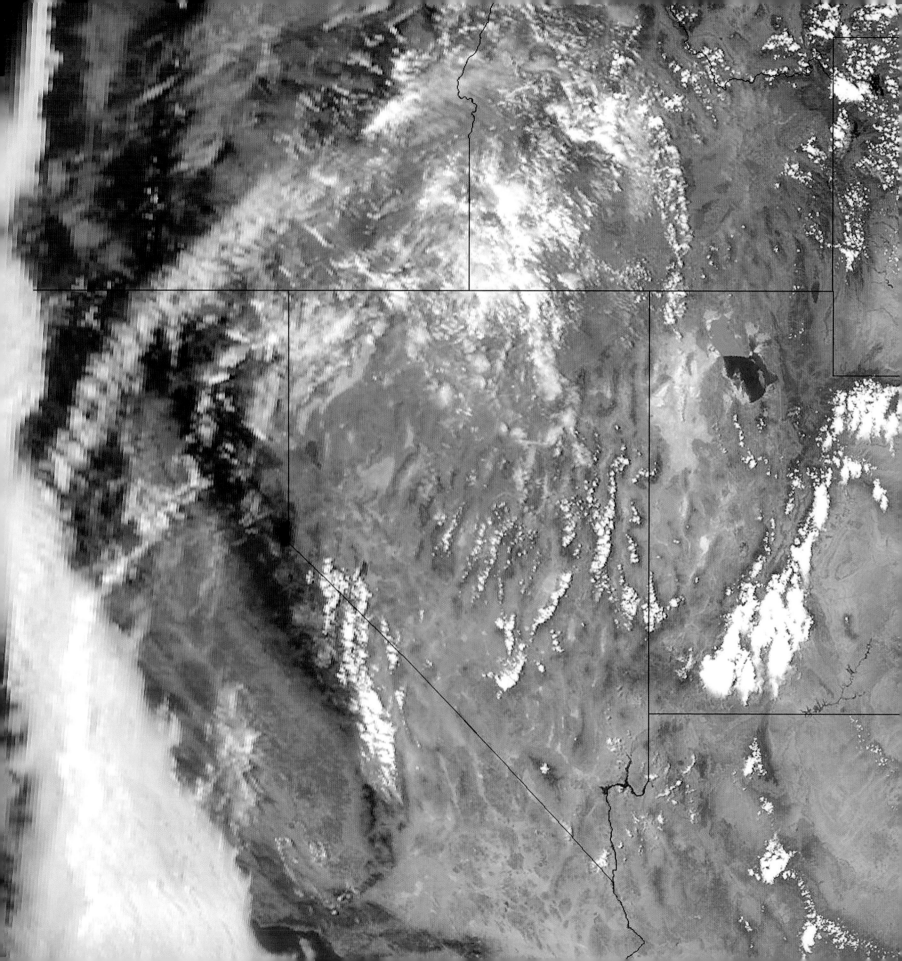

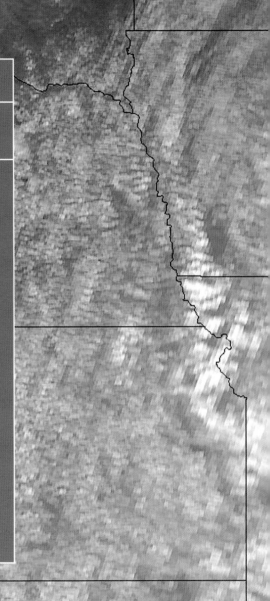

⇨ THE WEST

A HOST LISTING FROM
HURRICANEHOUSING.ORG

I am a single mom of a 10-year-old boy. I would love to help out another single mom with 1 or 2 kids. My son can sleep with me and his bedroom is available and we can make another bedroom in the basement. I offer warmth, love, and good home cooked meals to a family in need for as long as needed. I can provide for transportation to pick you up wherever you are if I can physically get to you by car. I want to be of service to a family in need. All my love and prayers,

LESLEE H.
TUCSON, ARIZONA

"WE NEVER THOUGHT WE COULD help. You watch stuff on TV, maybe give some money or whatever. But now, after this experience, I realize that actually doing something makes the more meaningful difference."

KAYANTAE SYNIGAL: When the hurricane came, I was pregnant and I just didn't want to leave. But it was a mandatory evacuation. We had to leave. So me and my fiancé and a bunch of friends of ours all put money in and rented a U-Haul truck. On our way out of the city, we picked up a bunch of families who had no transportation and put *them* in the back of the truck. So it was about twenty-five of us in the back of that U-Haul truck leaving New Orleans. And as we was leaving, we all looked out of the back—and the sky was just pitch-black from the storm. It was raining all over the place. I mean, we were just right ahead of the thing. It was like the storm was chasing us.

We made it up to Lake Charles. But it took us twelve hours to get there and it's normally like a two-hour drive. And, mind you, I'm pregnant. I'm sitting in the back of the U-Haul. I'm sitting in a chair from somebody's lawn or something like that. So, okay, twelve hours? In, like, a lawn chair. And when we got to Lake Charles—I was with my daughter, my fiancé and the other families we'd picked up—all of us checked into the Lake Charles Civic Center shelter. And as soon as I got there, I started dilating.

The hospital wouldn't keep me. I went and told them I was a high-risk patient because my first daughter was premature. She was born at thirty-two weeks. She was two pounds, two ounces. So I was a high-risk pregnancy and, I mean, as you can tell, I'm a little bitty person, so my immune system is not all that great. And I was basically telling them that, and they was like, "Oh, you're

fine, you're okay, dadadadada." And then I had to go back into the shelter and wound up getting sicker and started dilating even more. Then I started contractions. I started abdominal cramping. So I went back to the hospital. I had to beg someone from the Red Cross to give me a ride to the hospital to seek care. And when I got there, the people at the hospital said, "Oh, you're okay, dadadadada" and they sent me back to the shelter once again!

So then my fiancé, he was emailing people, trying to get us a place to stay, and we got a hotel room from FEMA. But they only paid for a few days. The doctors said I should stay there on bed rest, but we couldn't afford it and nobody would help us. I had doctor's papers saying that I'm on bed rest until it's time for me to deliver. But nobody would give us help so we could do that. So my fiancé, he's just typing away, going on the email and everything. And somehow he emailed Ms. Tobi and he told her my situation. Next thing you know I'm talking to her, and she said, "Come on, come to Phoenix. We'll pay for you. We'll provide a way for you to get down here."

TOBI HAWLEY: My heart went out to Kayantae. Because I'm a mom, and to have that kind of ordeal in the midst of childbirth—I couldn't imagine what she was feeling. I mean, there's no way she should've been discharged from the hospital the way she was.

KAYANTAE: She was so generous, and at just the time when I really needed it. Because I was really not feeling good. So I said to my fiancé, "What you want to do, honey?" And he was like, "I want to take this lady up on her offer." So we went from the hotel to the bus station, got a bus all the way to Houston, then connected in Houston to fly to Phoenix—a whole day traveling. I had never actually been on a plane before in my life. And now I'm pregnant, flying on a plane and dilating in the same day! It was crazy. And by the end, I felt all dizzy and sick. Real sick. But then Ms. Tobi met us at the airport.

[left to right] Rob Hawley (host), Beonce Synigal (evacuee's daughter), Tobi Hawley (host), Logan Hawley (host's son), Kayantae Synigal-Battle (evacuee & new mother), Amira Battle (evacuee's miracle baby), Kerry Battle (evacuee & new father), Benjamin Butler (evacuee)

TOBI: With tulips.

KAYANTAE: With some tulips! *(Laughs)* She was cute—so excited to see us. And I was just exhausted. My stomach was queasy. But it was so exciting to meet her. It felt great just to know that someone really cared and was really looking out for us.

TOBI: It wasn't anything special. We were watching like everybody else on the news everything that was going on with the hurricane. And I just thought it was terrible how unorganized everything was and that there were all these people there homeless in these shelters, with cots in a row. The shelter at Lake Charles had close to 5,000 people in it. And I mean, there was only one shower room with eight showerheads in the whole place for people to use. There was no privacy. They're sleeping right next to each other. And to be pregnant in that situation, I just can't imagine it.

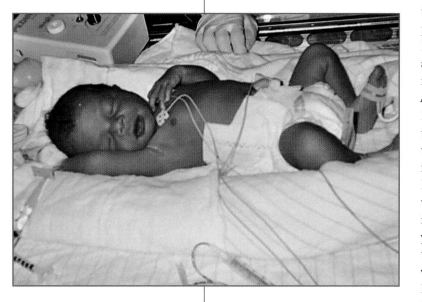

And we have this furnished seasonal rental that wasn't being used. I'm a real estate agent, and we have some rental properties. We have a lot of tourists who come to Phoenix, usually from December to April—that's the prime season. So I have a fully furnished rental, with all the linens, dishes, bedding, everything a family would need. And it stays vacant normally May to December. Because it's too hot. And I just felt bad. This place was sitting here vacant and somebody could be staying there. It's very nice in Phoenix. There are no hurricanes.

KAYANTAE: Right.

TOBI: The pictures I saw on TV—they disturbed me, as they did everybody. And I couldn't sleep. So I got up and started surfing the Internet. And that's where I found HurricaneHousing.org. There weren't many sites set up available to match people up with housing. The government had nothing set up. But HurricaneHousing had an easy-to-use system, by state and everything like that. I'd never heard of MoveOn before. But I just talked to Kayantae and I knew we had to help. And to me, I didn't care that they were strangers. They could've been bad people or good people; I was just trusting my faith. And I put a lot of trust in that. Because, I mean, this was a big deal. Her being pregnant and all? A big deal. And it just consumed me. I called everybody trying to get them flights. There were supposedly free flights available for the hurricane victims. But when you called Continental Airlines, they said you had to go through the Red Cross. They had vouchers, but no one knew how to get them. So when I called the Red Cross here, they told me to call the Red Cross in Louisiana. The Red Cross in Louisiana told me to call FEMA. FEMA told me to call the Red Cross. It was a big circle of calls, none of them giving me any luck. So I went the next morning to my church and I said, "I need your help. I need to get these people here. This lady's pregnant." And they immediately paid for the tickets. That's Northridge Community Church for you.

KAYANTAE: I have to thank them so much.

TOBI: Oh God, everybody here just wants to help. My OB/GYN volunteered to see Kayantae free of charge when she arrived. Kayantae got here on a Wednesday night and the next morning I already had a doctor's appointment set up for her.

KAYANTAE: Yes, tell them that...

TOBI: Well, we just thought it was gonna be a routine appointment. But when we went down to the doctor's, the next thing you know, people are scrambling around and people are on the phone, and they're like, "You need to take her over to the hospital right away. She's about to give birth!"

And they airlifted her. She was three to four centimeters dilated. So they airlifted her in a helicopter.

KAYANTAE: And I went from never bein' in the air my whole life to riding on a plane and a helicopter all in the same week!

TOBI: Your baby had frequent flier miles before she was even born. *(Laughs)*

And that's why I think her name is phenomenal. They're calling her Amira, after a miracle. And it is a miracle baby. That baby's been through quite the adventure before she ever even came into the world.

KAYANTAE: We had great guardian angels sitting over us. I think it's a blessing from God, just a blessing.

TOBI: Well, when you decide to help people, like I said, you don't know what kinda people you're gonna help. But we couldn't have asked for a better family or better people. Because they really want to make a difference in their lives and give back. It's amazing. They're just loving people. It's been really rewarding for us. It's changed our lives. We never thought we could help. You watch stuff on TV, maybe give some money or whatever. But now, after this experience, I realize that actually doing something makes the more meaningful difference. So it's been an education. And all of our friends and family are stepping up to the plate now. My uncle's in Houston volunteering now, because of what we've done. It's inspired a lot of folks. You know how everyone sits back wanting to do something, saying they'd like to do something, but they don't really do it? Well, look at us. We did something. And now everyone's coming around. It's amazing. It really is. ⇨

"BUT WHAT GOD IS SHOWING ME IS that we are still stable. You know? We're in another place, but still stable."

DWAYNE WILSON: I'm Dwayne Wilson. Yes sir. My name is Dwayne Wilson and this is my family. My wife is Lakesha Norbert, my son is Devon Norbert, my baby boy is Damoni Norbert and my oldest son is Larry Norbert. They ain't got their names changed into mine, but they are all my blood. And this is the true story of the Wilson family. This is our true story.

I never thought I would be leaving New Orleans. I've been there all my life, man. I was working for World Ship Supply as a forklift operator. We did everything for that ship. Whatever they needed for the ship to set sail, we provided for them.

Me personally, I have never traveled. Farthest I've ever been is Atlanta. I never thought I would be 2,000 miles away from New Orleans, living in Hanford, California. I always heard about California, but...here I am! I am actually living in Hanford, California. Man, it's truly a blessing and I just want to continue to praise God. Because this is where God put us. This is where Christ put us. And I am so surely content where I'm at right now.

My mother worked at Memorial Medical in New Orleans. Her employer let family members come stay there during the storm, so we rode the storm out there at the hospital and then managed to get home. The next morning, me and my kids woke up and heard on the radio that the flood gates at the 17th Street Canal broke. The water started coming into the city.

Before that water got to us, we managed to get back to the hospital and thought we would stay there. But the water rose up and filled the bottom of the hospital. So we volunteered to get the patients up out of there. We helped the nurses and the doctors evacuate the patients first.

During that process, word came down that *everybody* had to evacuate the hospital because the foundation of the hospital was starting to give way. So they managed to get everyone out of there and they brought us to a dry spot over on St. Charles and Napoleon. We stayed there for a few hours. And from there we got on a truck and they brought us to the New Orleans Convention Center. We stayed there for four days.

It was a long four days, man. But God is good. God provided a way for us to escape harm. I know all the horrors that were going on in that Convention Center. But me and my kids and my family, we didn't experience those horrors because we were busy trying to save ourselves. And like I said, God is the one. He is the one that protected us. We were kept safe, and I give credit to the Father. I just continued to pray that he would deliver us from the horrors of the Convention Center. And He did.

It...was bad there. I don't want to relive it.

After four days at the Convention Center, we managed to get through the gate and we caught a F150 Helicopter to the International Airport. From there, we flew to Fort Cafe Arkansas Military Base, and from Fort Café we managed to catch a bus to Fort Smith, Arkansas.

The pastor of the church in Fort Smith contacted a man named Mr. Andrew Kenny, who had an RV. Mr. Kenny offered to drive us all to California in that RV, and we happily accepted his offer. My wife had some friends in San Pedro, California and we thought we could stay with them. But his RV broke down on the way in Texas. He was so kind and generous to us, man. He said, "Well, look. The nearest bus station is in Amarillo, Texas, which is about thirty minutes from here." And he gave us all the money in his pocket so we could get bus tickets to California. Truly a blessing.

And somehow, through Mr. Kenny and his wife, Ms. Sandra, we ended up with this home here in Hanford. I

[back row, left to right] Stacy Crate (host), Lt. Travis Jones, USN (host's friend), Damoni Norbert (evacuee), Dwayne Wilson (evacuee); [second row, left to right] Lt. Cmdr. James Crate, Jr., USN (host), Patty Jones (host's friend), Larry Norbert (evacuee), Lakesha Norbert (evacuee); [front row] Devon Norbert (evacuee)

got a call from a lady named Ms. Heather Ryan and she said she had a great offer for us out in Hanford, California. I didn't know where Hanford was. And she said, "Well, I have a four-bedroom house for y'all free of rent for a whole year, plus a car." We gladly accepted, man. And this is where we wound up.

STACY CRATE: I saw on MSNBC where a lady in Austin had set up a home for some evacuees in San Antonio and I just thought we could do that too. So I went on the MSNBC website and clicked on the "how to help" button. It listed a whole bunch of different organizations that were linking people who needed homes with people who had homes. I just made a post on all the different websites. HurricaneHousing.org was one of them.

Then I was contacted by a lady in *Fresno*...who was in touch with someone in *Houston*...who called me and said that a family in *Arkansas* needed a home! So that's how it all happened. You put up a post and somehow a chain of people relay the message.

My husband is a Navy pilot with VFA-2. He and I are covering the rent on this house for Dwayne and his family for a full year. The King's County Board of Realtors is covering the utilities for a year. I've got a couple people that have offered to pick up a month's rent here and there. You know, my mother-in-law sent us the money to buy them a car. It's just a little bit of everybody pitching in to help, but it's mainly the people from my real estate office and a few of us military wives who have pulled this off.

DWAYNE: When we received this offer...I was just full of joy. *Full of joy.* Just to know that God is working for us, man. And He works for us *through people.* You know what I'm saying? These people out here truly opened their hearts with a sincerity to help. My heart goes out to every single one of them. From Mr. Kenny all the way to Stacy. God is good and I just continue to praise Him, man.

I feel like we're home. Another environment, sure, but it's home all over again. The love of these people that helped put this together, man. The unconditional love that they've shown us lets me know that this is home. Besides New Orleans, I mean, truly a *home.*

Right now, I don't know where we're gonna go from here and I'm not worried about it. Right now it's just about rejoicing in the contentment He's given us. We'll stay as long as God keeps us here. Me, I don't plan on the future no more. I make my plans by just trusting Him, the most high. However He works it out for us, that's how we're gonna go, man.

My kids and my wife, we all feel like we never left home. The same thing that was in us at home is still the same thing that's in us now. The Holy Spirit. God. This is the truth, man.

My kids were worried about getting back to school. But because of the love that's been shown us, they haven't missed a beat of school. They started back to school after only two days here. They are attending Preston Green Head Start and one goes to Pioneer Elementary.

And the kids that go to my sons' schools are very, very sensitive to what they've been through. They understand. They treat them so well, as if they had always known them. My sons fit right in with them, man, as if they had been here all their lives. It's beautiful.

STACY: We sent a press release to the local newspaper, the *Hanford Sentinel*, and eventually three articles got written up about them. They were on the front cover of the newspaper on Sunday. So a lot of people knew a little bit of what we were trying to do and the minute—the *minute*—we said we're trying to help a Hurricane Katrina family here, a lot of people opened up their hearts and gave stuff to help out.

DWAYNE: Truly amazing. Oh man, the community has opened up. It has opened up to us with such sincerity.

You know, we filed for all that federal stuff, everything that was required of us, at Fort Smith in Arkansas. We done been through that. And we never heard anything back. I still have money out there owed me from my job. We still have money out there from FEMA, I guess. All together, we probably have maybe $5,000 out there? I don't know how much it is. But right now, money is not the problem. Money is not the issue, man. There's the strictly unconditional love that people are showing us. I'm not worrying about nothin'.

I mean, I always been an independent man. I took care of my family at home. God knows I'm a workin' man. I had a good job. And my wife, she helped provide, too. We were pretty much stable. Then this disaster comes and you think it will destroy your life.

But what God is showing me that we are still stable, you know? We're in another place, but still stable. I thought I'd be a stranger in a strange land, but I feel right at home, man, for right now. Right at home. And it's beautiful.

I don't know how long it will take them to rebuild New Orleans. Our neighborhood has truly been destroyed. I can't look toward New Orleans right now. I just look toward the future. The future is forever. Looking back is never. So I'm going to continue to look forward. But from here, I know that wherever God puts us, that's always gonna be home. This is the gift that I've been given. We will always be home. ⇨

Stacy Crate carries Damoni Norbert.

"**W**HAT I'LL PROBABLY DO IS START cookin' for all these celebrities they've got out here. 'Cause I have actually been aspiring for some time to be a culinary chef. So I might try to be, you know, a private chef. It's either that or become a standup comedian."

SHAUNA SILIEZAR: The day before the hurricane turned into the Category Five, people started sayin', "Well, I guess we're gonna probably have to start thinkin' about, you know, leaving New Orleans or whatnot."

EILEEN GALINDO: But not you. (*Laughs*)

SHAUNA: No, yeah. Not me. (*Laughs*) Yeah, because, you see, I had to work that Saturday night, and I needed the money! I'm a bartender at Houston's. So, you know, they did mandatory evacuations that whole day Saturday, but I was like, "I gotta work." It actually took me about an hour-and-a-half to even *get* to work 'cause everybody's leavin' the city and I'm tryin' to go *into* the city to work.

Well, the night ended at about two in the morning. I got home and thought, *I need to just pack something up for me and the baby and just leave!* So I packed up and got my little baby and we went to Baton Rouge. I just drove my car. It was two in the morning and by that time people were off the roads. When I got to Baton Rouge I stayed at a lady's house...

EILEEN: Tell 'em how you found the lady.

SHAUNA: The lady was actually a bar guest from that night who had offered her place. She's in real estate and she had offered a place for me to stay with the baby if we didn't have anywhere to go. So that's how I got a place to stay in Baton Rouge. So thank God for her. And thank God I

went to work that night! But even though I felt lucky, that whole Sunday was very emotional. I mean I was very...I was freakin' out, I guess you could say. I cried a lot. I didn't know what was goin' on. You know? I only brought limited things for my baby and me. And my baby, she was kind of...she could probably sense that there was something going wrong. We're in a strange place with three big dogs. And I could hardly get in touch with any of my family because of the phone lines. I'm only twenty-six years old. And it was just the first time in my life I had to actually make huge decisions on my own without any kind of help.

The hurricane hit hardest that Monday. And my house got flooded and...and I couldn't go back. Everything was water-damaged and I didn't have renter's insurance. So pretty much that was it. My stuff is gone basically. So I decided I had to come out here to California. My husband—we're kind of separated. It's complicated. But he has a sister who lives near here in Thousand Oaks. And she was out of town that weekend, so she left the key for us to stay there. And I just jumped on the computer at her house and started tryin' to find a place to rent. And then, from linking, linking, linking, I got to the MoveOn.org site, and I saw the people offering rooms and places to stay for people who evacuated. So I just started emailing a whole bunch of those people. And Eileen was advertising that she had a place available for a couple months. So I just wrote to her and was pretty blunt in tellin' her my situation and what was goin' on. And I got a prompt response from her in like maybe three hours. She gave me her phone number and we met the next day—she was here with her friends cleaning up and getting the place ready. And people were bringing in donations. It was just...it was like a party!

EILEEN: It was insane.

[left to right] Shauna Siliezar (evacuee), Anjolina Siliezar (evacuee's daughter), Eileen Galindo (host)

SHAUNA: It *was* insane, yeah. You know, you live with a stranger and then strangers bringing stuff in to help you—it's wild.

EILEEN: All I did was send out an email to my friends here in L.A., mostly actors and industry people. I must have sent the email out to fifty people at most. But they forwarded it to their friends and to their friends and to their friends. And we ended up with people pulling up and, like, bringing their TVs, their furniture, their clothes and shoes, all this stuff. Everybody wants to help Shauna out.

We actually even ended up on this thing called the List, which goes to a collection of Hollywood muckity mucks. Apparently some powerful woman lawyer started it for bigwig industry folks who wanted to know that their donations would actually go directly to the people who needed them. I was only expecting a few of my friends to come by with, like, extra clothes. But instead, there were Jaguars pulling up, Porsches, you know, the whole nine yards. And these people would get out of their cars, carrying all sorts of very nice items and say, "Hello, I'm on the List." I thought they meant Craigslist. (*Laughs*)

SHAUNA: It was pretty amazing. And, you know, Eileen is the type of person who's very easy goin' from the initial, "Hi I'm Shauna, hi I'm Eileen" to a friendship, because she's just a very—I could just sense that she's a very giving and loveable person. So, that made it easy for me to be, you know, humble myself and be accepting of all these things that were comin' my way. Because for me, I just never had a situation in my life where I was at zero and I had to build myself back up. And having people help me do that, made me feel, I guess, special in a way. And if Eileen wasn't who she was, I probably wouldn't have felt so comfortable accepting all the donations and all the giving that people have done. And, well, it's great. I am so thankful for Eileen.

EILEEN: Oh—

SHAUNA: We spend a lot of time together.

EILEEN: We do.

SHAUNA: (*Laughs*) She makes good paella.

EILEEN: We went to the hat shop. Hung out with all my crazy actor friends.

SHAUNA: And she brought me to get shoes for my work. She showed me where I should go shopping. She told me about a grocery store called Trader Joe's that I'm gonna go check out today. So I'm really learnin' my way around, ya know?

I'm even already working—at the Houston's in Pasadena three days a week. I drive my car. I got my car and I'm actually trying to find child care right now, which is pretty hard in this town. I mean, Eileen is like—like if I run into a problem, I'm callin' Eileen about something. So—

EILEEN: Yeah, and that's fine. 'Cause it's hard.

SHAUNA: I don't have any girlfriends or any family here. I just have, you know, my husband—which is not even a normal marriage. I'm dealing with the fact that I had to move here from New Orleans. I'm also dealing with my husband, who I was separated from, and there are some issues with that. So, it's kind of a double whammy for me as far as my emotional state. But that's where Eileen comes in. And she's just a great person.

EILEEN: Isn't that swell?

SHAUNA: If my sister was here, I'd talk to her like I talk to Eileen. So, you know, it's a friendship.

EILEEN: Yeah.

SHAUNA: And it's not always easy here. There's hard stuff. L.A.'s huge compared to New Orleans. I mean, nine million compared to 1.2 million. That's a huge difference.

EILEEN: Oh, it is.

SHAUNA: There's not a lot of family-oriented things that I know of yet—parks, just being comfortable with the stroller. I mean, I'm in West Hollywood. I don't really know what that means, you know? I don't know what the area is like.

EILEEN: You're in East Hollywood.

SHAUNA: Oh, East Hollywood? See, I don't even know where I am, see what I mean? But, still, what gives me a good feelin' is...the South is known for its hospitality, right? I mean, if you ever visit New Orleans, you know that we're very kind, talkative, helping people. But you know what I've noticed since I've been here? I'm obviously in the right part of L.A. because I haven't experienced any selfishness. Everybody has been hospitable. And it does feel homey. It's not my home, but I do feel welcomed. In fact, I can't deny that there's a part of me that feels like I could really live here permanently.

I'm not totally adjusted yet, but this hasn't been as hard as I thought it was gonna be. Yes, I've been lonely. I've missed my family. But I'm trying to make my life here. I'm trying to find a school here for my daughter. I believe in this city. I mean, since I was young, California has always been stereotyped to me as this place of selfish people just out for themselves. So I got here not even thinking I'd be getting any donations. I was just gonna do it on my own and, you know, screw how hard it was.

And it's slow coming, but I know eventually I'll find what I'm looking for as far as childcare and work and schooling. Because I have aspirations of doing something more than being a server or bartender. I actually thought about being a comedian.

EILEEN: She actually went to an audition with me already.

SHAUNA: I actually—(*Laughs*)

EILEEN: She did.

SHAUNA: I was always told I was very funny and that I should be a comedian. But I'm more of a situational comic. I mean, I'm just funny. If something's funny, I'll make it funnier, that kind of thing. But I'm not sure I can be a comedian and get up there and do my own comedy. I'm not sure I know how to write the stuff, you know? Also, I don't think I'd be a good actress because I'm just funny. That's it. I could not be serious. I'm not a serious type of gal. I'm more of a fun person. So, probably tryin' to cry's gonna be real rough for me. And if you're gonna be a real actress, you have to be able to play a variety of different types of roles. You have to be able to be serious and cry and stuff. So I won't be goin' that route.

What I'll probably do is start cookin' for all these celebrities they've got out here. 'Cause I have actually been aspiring for some time to be a culinary chef. So I might try to be, you know, a private chef for these muckity mucks like you call 'em. It's either that or become a standup comedian. (*Laughs*)

EILEEN: Oh goodness, oh no! Well, you *did* go to an audition with me. I do a lot of voiceovers, so I had to go into my agent's office to lay down some tracks. And Shauna and her baby came with me. And it was sort of funny 'cause I'm used to going by myself or with my dog.

SHAUNA: Yeah, and I get there and someone gives me a food processor too.

EILEEN: That was pretty amazing. Shauna was just sitting there playin' with the baby or whatever. And the receptionist, Cindy, is like, "Oh who's that?" I said, "That's Shauna, the woman from Louisiana." Then everybody began to whisper. But it was great, because Shauna ended up with—well, her and Cindy are the same size.

SHAUNA: Yes.

EILEEN: So Shauna ended up replenishing her wardrobe from Cindy.

SHAUNA: Yeah, like a week after that, Cindy shows up at my door with a whole bunch of clothes.

EILEEN: Clothes that are actually wearable and totally Shauna's style.

SHAUNA: See what I'm talkin' about? I could really get used to this! (*Laughs*) ⇨

AARON LORENZ: It's important to have help in a situation like this. We were so surprised; we didn't think anyone would do something like this for strangers. I was touched. I was really moved by it. I mean, I'm not used to being in a situation where I have to ask for help. So that's obviously a little uncomfortable. But we're so grateful. It's so touching to see a civil organization do this. I mean, it's just the people doing it, right? ⇨

[left to right] Ashley Gable (host), Aaron Lorenz (evacuee), Renata Nascimento (evacuee)

A flooded neighborhood in New Orleans.

"SHE WAS ALREADY A REAL PERSON to them. And that seemed to give people such a desire to help."

LESLIE BENNETT: I left New Orleans with about fourteen members of my family—three generations in all. My grandmother is ninety-one and my little cousin is nine. We left a day before the hurricane hit. We packed up in about twenty minutes and just took off.

First we stayed at a shelter at the New Jerusalem Missionary Baptist Church in Jackson, Mississippi, sleeping on the floor. We ended up moving on to Bushkill, Pennsylvania because we have some family there. A cousin's house in the mountains. But I didn't like the mountains. I don't like the animals. They had deer and possums right in the front lawn that would come to the door and I'm like, "Nope. I'm a city girl!" I had to get out of there! Also being cooped up with my family for three weeks was enough for me. Fourteen other people? It's a mess.

My grandmother and aunt and my younger brother wound up going to Boston, and after they left, I called the Red Cross in Pennsylvania. And they gave me the website for HurricaneHousing.org. So I went to my cousin's computer and I started looking. I always wanted to see California. And so I thought, *This my chance.* And I started looking at a few of the listings and I emailed a few people. Steve was one of them. And it was a blessing I found the right one. Because it seems like it's a perfect fit to me.

STEVEN MORRISON: I'm a psychotherapist, but I spend most of my time in the mountains about two hours away working on my first book. I think Leslie and I exchanged one or two emails. Talked twice and I said, "Well, this feels like a done deal to me." She said, "Yeah, me too, right?" And I said, "Okay, I'm going to take the listing off." (*Laughs*) And then she made her...*little journey*. She found her own way out here.

LESLIE: I drove from Pennsylvania to Mississippi to pick up one of my best friends. And she drove with me to California. And she was like, "We're not stopping, we're going straight to Cali." And we drove all the way here in twenty-six hours. But we got lost in California...or Arizona...or... well, it was in the desert. We couldn't find this place. I've never been out this way before!

STEVEN: I had no idea where she was. And the phones would never work. Or they'd work for just a second. So I had no idea really where she was for most of the time. Finally, she called and said, "Well, we're here, we're three hours away." I said, "Oh, all right, where are you?" And she named a place about eight hours away from here!

LESLIE: It was okay until we got to the desert and then when we saw the mountains, it was getting dark and we was just lost.

STEVEN: They got here at two in the morning, and I just let them fall asleep, you know? I'm not going to come bother them. So two the next afternoon, I'm like, "Knock, knock,—you still alive?" And she comes out and she's all decked out in high heels like this, and I said, "You have no idea where you are, do you?" I mean, this is the beach!

LESLIE: I am coming from a place where I'm not used to walking at all! New Orleans is flat. And so I had my heels on, and we're walking around and I'm like, "What is this?" And I kept going up and oh my God, it's a hill.

STEVEN: (*Laughs*)

LESLIE: He thinks it's very funny. (*Laughs*) That's our little rapport right there. Yeah. (*Laughs*) We get along. He's an angel.

STEVEN: It's just been an amazing experience, this thing.

LESLIE: He's amazing. He's been so generous.

STEVEN: It's not just me. I emailed Leslie before she arrived and asked, "What size clothing do you wear?" And I just sent out an email to local people right here in the South Bay, describing Leslie's story and then I said, "If you have

[left to right] Leslie Bennett (evacuee), Steven Morrison (host)

anything to donate, please do." And the outpouring that I got as a result of that! All of a sudden everyone I sent it to—which was less than fifteen people I think—had sent this email all over the place. I mean it ricocheted to New York and back, with job offers and all kinds of stuff. So I spent all day Saturday and Sunday either going and meeting people and collecting stuff or being here while people dropped stuff off. I didn't want to overwhelm Leslie when she arrived, but I could have covered the room down there with stuff that people had brought.

I was just stunned at the response. I mean, they didn't know her; they didn't even see a picture of her. But they knew her name was Leslie, she was twenty-eight years old and she was coming here from the hurricane. She was already a real person to them. And that seemed to give people such a desire to help. So many people said it to me, "This feels so much better than just writing a check." This one woman brought me fifteen bags worth of stuff! Clothing and other stuff she had been collecting from several other people, all for Leslie. I tried to keep track of it all but at a certain point you just couldn't.

LESLIE: It surprised me. When we came in, that first day I was here? I got up and we came down downstairs, and we went through the apartment. I went to put my few things in the closet, but the closet was already full! Of clothes, shoes, even perfume and makeup! I mean, anything and everything.

STEVEN: And a lot of people were like, "Does she need TVs and dishes and furniture?" And all I could say was, "Wow."

LESLIE: It was overwhelming at first, but I'm so grateful for it.

STEVEN: You can tell she's settling in.

LESLIE: I actually have two job interviews today. Office work, so far. One of the girls who gave me some things—her name is Gianna—she keeps calling to check on me. And it's funny. I've never actually physically met her. She came from Steven's email. And she now has an interview set up for me through her sister that works at Prudential! Isn't that something? I mean, we've never met face to face or whatever, but she's recommending me and she calls me almost every day too.

Gianna. I mean, she's like family now. She says, "Are you okay?" And I say, "Yeah I'm okay." And I am. I'm gonna be just fine. ⇨

MAX HOFFMAN: Having Maurice here is kind of like having a new little brother. He's seven, so I play with him a lot. I'm twelve. I'm in the eighth grade. We just play games and stuff.

MAURICE EVANS: Yeah. It's like a little adventure or something. I get scared sometimes but what I got to do is be patient. And I'm learning to be patient. Sometimes being scared, it goes away. I like my new school. They're building us a new playground. One more piece and then it's finished. I can't wait. ⇨

[back row, left to right] Jon Hoffman (host), Diane Evans (evacuee);
[second row, left to right] Hannah Hoffman (host's daughter), Carmen Evans (evacuee);
[front row, left to right] Maurice Evans (evacuee), Max Hoffman (host's son)

"PEOPLE CONFUSE THE GOVERNMENT with the citizens."

ALEX SILVA: I'm from Rio de Janeiro. I was a writer in Brazil and I got invited for the Ph.D. program at Tulane, the Spanish and Portuguese program. I arrived in New Orleans exactly two weeks before the evacuation. So I pretty much had time to do nothing else but meet my boss, walk around campus and get my bureaucracy in order, you know? I got my Social Security card and my first paycheck the day before the hurricane. (*Laughs*) And I mean, I was watching the news. I knew that something was happening with the weather. But I really had no idea how bad. I don't think anybody did. It didn't hit the news, really, that this was something very, very serious, until Saturday morning.

So I was just thinking about school, you know: *When I start classes on Monday, my new life will be in full swing.* That was Friday. I went to sleep thinking that my future for the next few years was pretty much set. The next day I woke up and I had to evacuate. Our plan for that day was that my roommate was going to fumigate the house and I was going to take some time off with the dogs—my dog and his dog. But when I woke up, my roommate was just staring at the TV, freaking out and saying, "We have to go *now*. This is big."

My roommate and his dog and his girlfriend were going to Houston in his car. So I asked if I could go with them. And the guy said *no*, man! No, because there's nowhere to stay where they were going. And I was just dumbfounded. I was thinking, *Oh my God, I'm new here, I don't know anyone. My roommate is bailing on me.* Crazy, you know? So I called my boss. He had a four-month-old baby to take care of, and the guy was going crazy. He couldn't talk. He said he was gonna call me back but never did. That's when I realized, *oh, man, I'm totally on my own.*

Now, this happened to be orientation week at my university, so the president of Tulane was addressing the students and the parents. All the parents of all the freshmen were in New Orleans that day to help their kids move into their dorms and apartments. So instead of giving his usual welcoming address, the president basically gave out instructions on how to evacuate the city. He said that Tulane was going to offer us buses to bring us to Mississippi. We would stay in the gym at Jackson State University for two or three days and then we'd go back to New Orleans and everything was gonna be nice. He was actually telling the parents not to worry about sending their kids away and to think of the whole thing as a type of "field trip." Oh, man! (*Laughs*)

So I decided to go with the Tulane buses. But to do that, I had to leave my dog Oliver behind. They wouldn't let me bring him. So I locked the doors and windows. I left him two buckets of water and four pounds of dog food and that was that. I said goodbye and told him I'd be back.

The bus on the way up was almost like a party. Because we were on a "field trip," right? People just weren't taking the storm seriously. But once we got to the gym at Jackson State, and everyone started seeing what was happening on TV, they began to get really nervous about how bad this thing actually was. All *I* could think about was my dog. Oliver was basically trapped, you know? He had enough water, but who knows what was going on with him? Who knows when would I be able to go back to him? I was facing the very, very likely prospect that he would starve to death. And there was nothing I could about it. I was frantic.

And so after just one night at the shelter I called my sister in California and she offered to fly me out there. Her husband is a Ph.D. student in Berkeley and she works in San Francisco. We were already trying to see if I could I spend a semester there. So, in a way, I just arrived early.

[left to right] Alexander Silva (evacuee), David Weitzman (host)

(*Laughs*) And then I ended up living here in Berkeley with David.

DAVID WEITZMAN: I got an email from MoveOn asking for volunteers to help the evacuees, so I went to the website and filled in the application. About thirty seconds later I got a response from them. Alex must have called me two minutes later.

ALEX: I can't thank him enough. I was completely freaking out. I had been lucky enough to be able to stay with my sister for a while. And then I found out that Oliver was actually rescued in New Orleans. I was so relieved that he was okay. But that meant that I had to find a new place to stay, because my sister lives in a very small apartment where they allow no dogs.

So I started looking for apartments. And the prices were just absolutely huge. This area is expensive, especially with a dog. So I was getting kind of desperate. I mean, honestly, I'm kinda broke now. So when someone told me about HurricaneHousing.org, it gave me some hope. I filtered my search down to places that were dog-friendly. And when I saw David's ad, it caught my eye. It was the ad with the least amount of information I've ever seen.

You didn't write *anything*. (*Laughs*) You just wrote yes, dog-friendly, welcome, whatever. I only called you because I was desperate! I was calling every single one that said dogs are welcomed.

DAVID: I'm not that particular. In fact, I think Alex was more particular than me. (*Laughs*) His major concern besides the dog seemed to be to assure me that he wasn't a serial killer. (*Laughter*) He provided me with a lot of documentation: his Tulane student card, his visa and passport, his driver's license, every piece of identification he had.

ALEX: I'm a Brazilian. We don't trust easily. At least not Brazilians from Rio.

DAVID: Maybe I'm naive, but I really had no qualms about letting a stranger into my house. None at all. I mean, I didn't particularly *want* to have a serial killer, but Alex assured me he wasn't one, so...

ALEX: We bonded.

DAVID: I had a dog who died a couple of months ago.

ALEX: Oliver is very happy because he inherited a lot of stuff.

DAVID: (*Laughs*)

ALEX: I'd left New Orleans with nothing. I mean, I'd really thought we were leaving just for the weekend, you know? So to find a place like this, that's already set up for a dog to live in, it's just great for Oliver—and for me. I mean, you just can't imagine how important Oliver is to me. Really, for anyone, their pets can be so important in times like this.

DAVID: That's true. One of the things that I've come away with from this experience is a realization of the enormous pull of animals. For instance, on television this morning they showed a woman, probably in her sixties or seventies, who absolutely refused to evacuate because she couldn't take her pet. And there was another woman they showed pulling a horse trailer with her car on the highway. She wouldn't abandon her horses. And they ended up having to camp under a bridge because their car had broken down and she couldn't gallop the horses on the freeway or pull the horse trailer anymore. I don't know if I would've been able to understand that kind of thing before meeting Alex. But he's brought these feelings home very clearly. And I can see that he's not unique in this area. The importance of people's pets is something I once might've dismissed, but not anymore.

ALEX: And my story is like a miracle, you know? The dog was locked in for a week and a half. He stayed there, home alone, for nine days. The house was entirely crapped of course—dog crap everywhere. (*Laughs*) But Oliver is a street dog. I actually found him in one of Rio's major slums. That's why he's so tough. Still, if the house had flooded it wouldn't have mattered how tough he was. But we were lucky. The house was intact. No windows were broken; no glass was broken. And because my apartment's on the second floor, it wasn't flooded. A guy broke into the house and rescued the dog and, you know, thank God for him. That guy is my hero. I want to do what he does someday—animal rescue. I want to volunteer.

DAVID: (*Laughs*) I think he might.

ALEX: I mean, people like that are inspiring. This dog rescue guy even checked around my apartment and gave me a report that all my stuff is still there and in good shape. Of course there's nothing there anyone would be willing to steal. It's only books and papers and clothes. I mean, I'd like to get it all back eventually. But now my roommate is threatening to throw my things on the street if I don't pay rent. I told him, "I'm not paying rent. I don't have money. I'm not living there. I'm sorry." And in fact, that's one of the major concerns of the hurricane evacuees—all the landlords that are asking for rent. And people are saying, "I can't pay." One, because they have no money and no job. And two, because they're already probably paying a new rent wherever they're living now. So I don't know how this thing is gonna get solved, but it's gonna continue to be a problem.

DAVID: And you've got your own problems. (*Laughs*)

ALEX: You know, I have a blog back home in Brazil. And it's very interesting, because I told my story in my blog and it had some repercussions in the Brazilian media. I kinda became one of the faces of Brazil for the hurricane. Many people read my blog and called me, asking for interviews. And everyone kind of judged me, you know? There was a big debate on whether I was an asshole or not because I left the dog behind. People were calling me names and telling me I should never have a dog, that I should never have a son, because I was a monster, etc. They really got into it.

And it really bothered me, you know? Because, let me tell you, if I had known the hurricane was gonna be one-third as bad as it was, I would have taken my dog and hopped on the first plane Saturday morning to California. But back then no one thought it was gonna be that bad.

We all thought we were going for a weekend out. I just had no idea. Now I'm making sure to let people know that that my dog is here and doing well. I even posted pictures of him playing in the yard out back. In Brazil, everyone is still following our story as if it were some kind of soap opera. (*Laughs*)

DAVID: It's a very interesting phenomenon.

ALEX: You know, it *is* interesting. In Brazil and most of the rest of the world, partially because of Mr. Bush, Americans are not really liked as much as they used to be. People confuse the government with the citizens. I've always known Americans because I was educated in the American school back home. I know this country for a long time and I came here because I like it. But people back home, when I tell them what's going on here, they don't believe. They just think, *Oh, those capitalists, those leeches, those pigs, they live on exploiting the riches of the world*. And I tell them I've never seen anything like that.

In fact, I'm almost overwhelmed by goodwill I've found here. Everyone is reaching out, from MoveOn to Berkeley to the companies that donated gift certificates. It's really, really amazing. And when I tell my readers how I feel about eventually going back to Brazil, I say it's going to be tough. Because the first time someone starts bad-mouthing Americans, I'm gonna feel really inclined, to…well, usually I would just ignore them. But right now, I'd feel like punching them in the face. Because the people who say these bad things about Americans, they just don't know what they're talking about.

They just don't know. ⇨

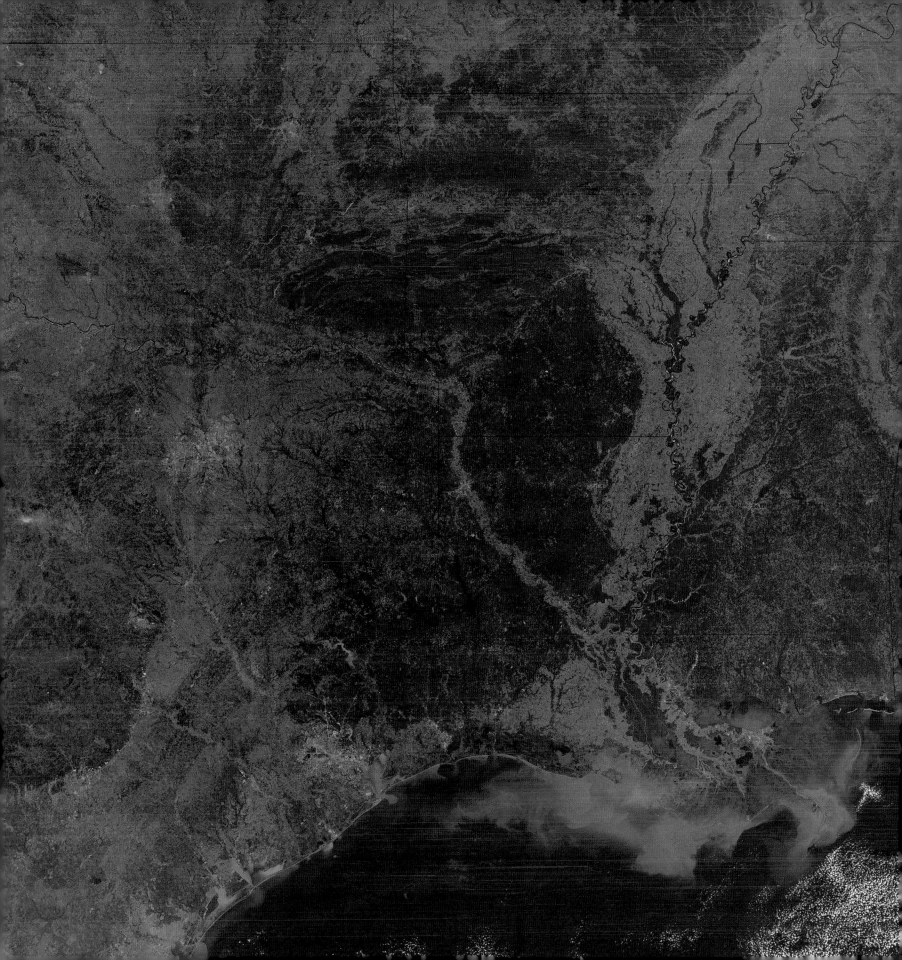

⇨ THE SOUTH

A HOST LISTING FROM
HURRICANEHOUSING.ORG

We are a loving family that would treat you like you were our family. We have a dog and 2 cats. We will take singles, family or children. We are close to schools and will help you find a job. We have an extra bedroom and can always find a place to put more mattresses if needed. God bless you all.

KIM C.
ASHLAND, KENTUCKY

"I KNOW FROM EXPERIENCE WHAT IT'S like to have everything in order and then have it all just fall apart overnight."

RANDY CAMPBELL: I'm retired. Disabled, actually. And where my girlfriend Regina and I live, in Glencoe, Alabama, we're pretty isolated, pretty much in the woods, ya know what I mean?

So when I turned on my TV and saw all the horror that Katrina was dealin' out in New Orleans—seeing all these people losing their homes—it seemed as if it could be happening a world away. I mean, physically we're only a few hundred miles apart. But the experience I was having sitting in my living room in Glencoe just could not have been further apart from what these people were going through in this city just six or seven hours away by car. But watching the news—watchin' all these peoples' lives being literally swallowed up overnight and no one there to help—it just brought tears to my eyes and touched me in such a personal way.

I recalled the time that I was put out of *this* house. I'd had a very bad accident. I was cuttin' down a tree in the woods and the thing fell on me. It hit me right in the face and did damage that would've amounted to $22,000 in medical bills. The thing is, I had no medical insurance at the time. With the mortgage on my house I just couldn't afford to pay it any longer. And of course, with the severity of my accident I was put out of work. And then I couldn't pay my mortgage. So the bank foreclosed on me. And they ruined my credit so I couldn't borrow money to have the emergency dental work done that I needed.

I was literally forced to do the dental work myself. And believe me, I am not a dentist. But I had no choice. I had no choice but to file down my own teeth. They'd been broken up into jagged edges to the point where they were causin'

me unbearable pain. So I fixed the damage myself, sittin' right there at my kitchen table. It was not a pretty sight, believe you me.

Fortunately, I was able to find a lawyer who saved me from being evicted from my home. That was just a blessing from the good Lord. I was led to individuals who were able to help me reestablish this home and bring these people from the bank into a court of law for what they'd done to me. So I just thank God for that. Honestly, if not for God watching over me, I'd be out in the cold right now.

My point in tellin' this story is that I feel like I know from experience what it's like to have everything in order and then have it all just fall apart overnight. I felt like I could relate to what these people in New Orleans were going through. And I remembered that when I was saved from the misfortune I'd endured, I'd made God a promise. I said, "Lord, if there's ever anything I can do to repay the gratitude that you've given me by helping someone else, I will."

So when we saw the HurricaneHousing Internet site address come up on Fox News, we emailed right away with the offer to take someone in. Regina and I said, "We don't have any money, but we've got space. This is a two-family house. Let's put it to use." And shortly after we sent that email, a shelter in San Antonio called and said, "We have two people for you."

MYRA DAVIS: We had just registered for HurricaneHousing a day earlier. And then the next thing you know, the Red Cross gave us a voucher and we were headed to Glencoe on a Greyhound bus. We left at eight o'clock that night and got here the next day at six p.m.

JAMES DAVIS: It was a twenty-two-hour ride. Very long.

MYRA: We had a lot of time to think. Honestly, I was afraid to be going to a stranger's house to live.

JAMES: You *were* afraid! Myra couldn't stay in her seat for the whole bus ride. She kept on gettin' up and walkin' around. But there was really nowhere to go. I mean, we were on a bus! (*Laughs*) Me, I had some apprehension. But

[left to right] James Davis (evacuee), Regina Willis (host), Myra Davis (evacuee), Randy Campbell (host)

once we got here and met Randy and Regina and started talkin', we just seemed to bond instantly. We were comfortable with each other right from the start.

REGINA WILLIS: It was like they were coming home to family.

JAMES: And now we've been here for almost two weeks. And it's goin' really well.

RANDY: It's been a wonderful experience. I could not have hand-picked two better people. I just feel lucky to have the opportunity to extend the kind of hospitality to James and Regina that the Lord gave to me. I could tell they were very nervous when they got here. They even told me that they were scared. And I just said, "Well, you have nothing to be afraid of. You're welcome here."

REGINA: When we discussed the idea of putting our home up, I told Randy, "I feel God has plans for our lives to cross paths with someone in need and to share whatever he has in store." And when the shelter called and said they had two people for us who were currently staying at the San Antonio shelter in Building 1536, I couldn't help but notice that "1536" are the last four digits of our phone number.

JAMES: (*Laughs*) True.

REGINA: So it was like a sign from God! (*Laughs*)

JAMES: Honestly, I can believe that. I mean, right now we're just taking it one day at a time. And we do hope to get back to New Orleans to, you know, check out our property and see what's salvageable. If anything is. ...

MYRA: But we think we're going to end up making our home here, in Glencoe, from now on.

JAMES: Yeah, we've made the decision to relocate here. Before the hurricane, Myra and I had actually been talking about moving to somewhere new. We just hadn't made up our minds. And when Katrina came along, that kind of gave us an unexpected boost, to say the least. (*Laughs*)

And I'm gonna be honest with ya. I don't think I could have found a better place to go. Because I've been treated like I've been here all my life, like I was born here. Everybody that I've met has just gone so out of their way to be nice. And it's not a pretense. This is a down-home, from-the-heart feelin' that I've gotten from everybody I've

met since I've been here. It's a good feelin'. It's a really good feelin'—especially after all we've been through.

Back home in New Orleans, we were basically at Ground Zero when the storm hit. We lived in a neighborhood called Little Zion, which is in what you'd call the Mid-City area. And when the levee broke and the flood of water started comin', it went straight to our neighborhood.

Myra was at work; she worked at the local school's cafeteria. I used to be a merchant seaman, but I'm retired now, on disability. Anyhow, when the floods started, Myra managed to get right home. And then we set out to go to the Superdome.

MYRA: But we never made it there.

JAMES: Went to a bridge nearby our house. It was the highest ground. There were messages on the radio telling us to go there. Supposedly, if we went there, we'd be transported to the Dome. But instead we got stuck on that bridge—sitting there, outside, exposed to the elements for five days.

And what made it worse, the city government had been moving prisoners, from one penitentiary to another, and they were all stuck there on that bridge with us.

MYRA: Everyone was worried that the situation was gonna get...well, you know, violent or out of control.

JAMES: I mean, it would've been a perfect opportunity for one of these prisoners to do something desperate and try to escape. Thank God they didn't. The guards kept them at the other end of the bridge for the whole five days and there was never a problem. We had no interaction with those prisoners. But it was tense. They could see us and we could see them, but we all just kept to ourselves.

Luckily we were with our neighbors. We lived in a complex with four apartments and most of the people stuck on the bridge came from there. We just all got together and tried to make the best of it. Different people had food—little cans of sausages, stuff like that. Everybody took a little bite of this, a little bite of that. There were some crackers and peanut butter goin' around for quite some time as I remember.

The food and water had totally run out, though, by the time the military helicopters finally showed up at

Survivors arrive at New Orleans airport for medical treatment and evacuation to other states.

the end of the week. We were airlifted to New Orleans International Airport and spent the night there, sleeping on the floor. After that we were put into buses and transferred to what I guess you would call a staging center, in San Antonio, Texas. After a few days there, we were put into a shelter at what used to be Kelley Air Force Base, at a different location in San Antonio. We were there for about a week and a half, maybe two weeks. But it seemed like forever. Just in a big room, sleeping on the floor with hundreds of other people.

And then a lady in charge of finding shelter and housing for the evacuees asked if we wanted to relocate. And we told her yes. She was actually the one who went on the Internet and found Randy and Regina, who agreed to take us in. And two or three days later, we were in a Greyhound bus terminal in Glencoe, rattled out of our minds, and Randy was pickin' us up with a big, friendly smile on his face.

And from that point on, as I said, we've just felt so blessed. I mean, the outpouring of love and humanity we've been shown—it's something that's changed our lives already in so many ways. And I honestly feel that the only way I can repay this type of love is for me to be there as well, for someone else, in their time of need.

Right now, Myra and I are focusing on trying to locate some of our relatives from New Orleans who've gone missing. I have an uncle who lived in the Ninth Ward—one of the hardest hit areas. I spoke with him about a day before the storm. But I haven't heard anything from him since. And I have a sister who's in Wisconsin. But she doesn't know where I am and I have no idea how to get in touch with her. All my phone numbers are underwater somewhere, back in New Orleans. I hope that by the time people read this book that I'll have found my family. But right now I just don't know how I'm gonna do it. I've tried

every avenue I can think of, but nothing's worked so far. I even tried writing Oprah a letter.

MYRA: But in the meantime, we're trying not to let our fears go to our heads. We are just trying to have faith that the people we love are okay, just like us. We're even tryin' to behave in the semblance of a normal life every now and again. We've gone out to dinner with Randy and Regina two or three times. That was really nice.

RANDY: The way I feel is that Regina and I can be family for James and Myra while they try to find their own. Even though we may not be of the same ethnic background, I believe we've developed a permanent family bond with each other that will never be separated by race or color. It's real. Our doors stay open. There's no asking, "Can we come up here or can we go down there?" We're just like brothers and sisters.

JAMES: Like one big happy family.

REGINA: My four-year-old granddaughter lives with Randy and I. And every morning after she gets dressed she says, "I've got to go check on Ms. Myra and James!" (*Laughter*)

RANDY: We're there for each other. I may be carrying Myra and James right now. But I truly believe that if something happened to me—if I were to lose my home—they'd be there to help me. And I truly hope they stay here as long as they want.

They've come to me and asked, "Can I help you with money or anything like that?" And I said, "Well, I'm very thankful for the kindness, and if you want to you're welcome to. But if you're not able to, that's not a problem either." Because it's not a money thing. We're here because the Lord's been good to me.

I mean, if these folks never had a penny, I had rather have *them* here in my house than to be renting to someone for seven or eight hundred dollars a month. Because the bond we have—money can't buy that kind of bond.

JAMES: All the same, we're really looking forward to the time when we can contribute our fair share and get back on our feet financially. As of now, as far as funds go, we haven't even gotten any federal assistance. We went down to the Red Cross and they gave us an introduction to some of the charitable organizations in the city. And we are dealing with FEMA, but it's been a month and we still haven't seen any fruit from that.

Luckily, I still receive a disability check every month. So that takes a little bit of the pressure off. But basically, that's about it.

And, I mean, our car got lost in the hurricane so even trying to get out for a job interview is a challenge. I've tried to file an insurance claim so I can use the money to buy a replacement vehicle. But the insurance company said, "We can't pay you anything because your policy doesn't cover acts of God." And I'd really like to check on whether or not that's true. But my paperwork is in the glove compartment of my car, which is under water. So the transportation issue has been a challenge to say the least. But we'll surmount it.

RANDY: You can use one of my cars to go anywhere you need to go. Here are the keys!

Seriously, I know James and Myra would feel more comfortable if they had transportation that officially belonged to them. But as I said, it's just not a problem to use what's on offer here. And that statement has no fine print.

JAMES: The one thing that just amazes me and fills my heart with hope amidst all of this is—the one thing I keep going back to in my mind—is that time spent stranded on the bridge in New Orleans. Five days. It wasn't so much about us. My main concern was more with the elderly people who were stuck up there. A lot of those old folks, they didn't have their medication. And they were out in the hot sun and pouring rain and winds, twenty-four hours a day for five days straight.

MYRA: And everybody, everybody was...

JAMES: Everybody did their part in taking care of each other. That's the one thing I would like everyone to know: that in a time of need and desperation, people came together. And they helped each other. ➪

DONA EDWARDS: This is the first year I've been involved with MoveOn.org and their campaigns. I signed up for HurricaneHousing right away, but I definitely wanted to err on the side of safety. I wanted to have a comfortable feeling about the person I allowed in my home. Originally, I thought that I'd probably just house a woman—unless it was someone really exceptional. I just thought, "I dunno. A guy? I dunno." And then I met Vincent and I'm like, "Oh well. It's Vincent! No problem." *(Laughs)* And now I kinda like having him around, believe it or not. ⇨

[left to right] Dona Edwards (host), Vincent Marini (evacuee)

"NOTHING CAN BE WORSE THAN waking up and everything you have is gone. Only thing worse would be dying but at least then you'd be in heaven."

MELANIE JAMES: I reside in New Orleans at 5436 Chartres, better known as the lower Ninth Ward or the C2C, across from the Industrial Canal. I've been a dental assistant there for the last seven years, lived a pretty normal life. I have two daughters, Brionne and Milan Miller, eleven and nine years old. They attended public school in the lower Ninth Ward. I lived and worked in the Gentilly area, not too far from the Lakefront. Everything was pretty normal routine, everyday living.

I remember hearing on the news that the storm was coming. My aunt stayed on a street, ironically called Flood Street, which is a block away from my house, in a two-story home. So we figured, well, even if the water rises she can go up in the attic. I have two daughters. They evacuated the Friday before the storm with their father in Mississippi, so I knew that they were okay. Me and their dad aren't together anymore, so they left with him and his wife.

I myself went to my friend Leroy's home on the other side of the Canal. It's still the Ninth Ward, but I thought I would be safe there.

About 4 a.m. Monday morning, I woke up. There was no electricity, the lights were already out and we could hear the wind gusting. I thought, *God, what's going on?* So we stepped outside on the porch and up the street you could see something approaching. It was a refrigerator— a refrigerator floating down the road in some sort of tidal surge of water, debris and water just roaring in. Water was falling from the sky.

And I said, "Oh my God, that's not rain." Because you can smell the water and you can taste the water. I mean, if you're from New Orleans you know the difference between the rain and the lake and the canal. It all smells different, it tastes different. I'm like, "God, that's the *lake*."

We went to the first floor and began putting sand bags by the front door. The water had already started coming in, so my friend suggested that we get stuff off the floor. And so we went into the adjacent bedroom and started putting things on top of the dresser. And when we turned around that water was to our *knees*. I remember saying, "We've been out here like an hour." Leroy said "No, Mel, it's only been twenty minutes."

I told him, "We're gonna drown."

It's only been twenty minutes and the water's already up to our knees? We're gonna drown.

And all I can think is, *Where's all this water coming from?* I thought it was only gonna be five to ten feet of water. The storm is passing east of the city so we shouldn't have been hit by heavy rain, heavy flooding, any of these things. So we went upstairs and we began gathering items. They said on the news to make sure you have a hammer, something that you can break through the roof with in case you need to break out of the attic. So we found a hammer.

Within the first hour of the storm, the entire first floor was covered with water. So we made a marker on the second floor wall where we were, and decided that once the water gets to this level, then we're gonna have to move to the attic. A one point I was gathering items and I was looking out the window and I saw the roof rip right off the house next door. It just ripped right off. And I just started panicking.

There was a woman and a child who was with us, who Leroy rescued because her roof had collapsed on her. Well, we had heard her screaming for help. So he took a tire, swam through the water and put her baby,

[left to right] Melanie James (evacuee), David Eichler (host's brother), Ellen Lytle (host)

a one-year-old child, inside of the tire and brought them back to his home.

At this point, the water was almost up to the second floor of the house. All the windows were blown out, so the wind was rushing through the house, and the water started dumping into the house through the open windows.

We went up to the attic. We're all standing there in the attic, listening to the water rise, hanging onto a hammer. And that attic had a storm roof with big orange rust stone shingles, so even with a hammer, how you gonna break out?

By Monday night, we can see helicopters flying. We lit a chair on fire on the porch to try to get their attention. But they were flying across the canal, by the lower Ninth Ward, which was adjacent to where I was. I was like, "Why aren't they stopping?" They didn't stop.

Tuesday morning we can see people starting to wade through the water. The water was real black. A lot of oil and gas or whatever it was in it and dead animals. It just gave you a real dark eerie feeling. I saw some army trucks about three blocks down on St. Claude Avenue. And I'm yelling to the neighbors, "Where are the army trucks going?" And they said, "Well, in order for you to get help you gotta swim to them, because they can't come up the streets where we are." So I swam down St. Claude Avenue to a school where the army trucks were picking people up. I'm not sure how deep the water was, but it was definitely more than ten feet.

I just swam. There were downed power lines, so I avoided them. It was very scary because I couldn't see through the water. The water was black and dirty. At that point I was by myself. I chose to leave the home where I was with my friend. I wanted to go to the Superdome, because I thought I'd feel safer at the Superdome. You know,—we're in this home, we don't have any food, we don't have any water and the water is still rising. Seemed safer to go to the Dome.

I didn't know at this point where my family was, because I left my mom, my two aunts and my uncle across the canal in the lower Ninth Ward.

I just figured being across the canal, because of the levee breaching, you know, what if the levee breaks? How

we gonna get out? There's no way we could cross over to St. Claude Bridge to get on the other side. My family had stayed, so at that point, I pretty much assumed that my family dead, to be honest with you. I assumed my family dead.

So I got to the truck pick-up. And they transported us to the Superdome, just riding on the trucks through the city. Seeing the devastation that had taken place within a matter of hours, it...it was horrific.

You could see people wandering on the sidewalks looking for help, and I was hoping that they could have come with us, you know, because there was just a sense of lostness on everyone's face. Their faces seemed to say, "What do we do? Where do we go, where is the help? How did you all get on a truck?" People literally screaming, "Can we come with you?! Help! Help! I want to get on!" But you had to get to these particular meeting spots in order to be picked up to be transported to the Superdome. It's not like they were just driving by and picking people up on the street, so you actually had to know about them and get to them.

When I walked through the doors of the Superdome I instantly began crying. Because I could see the chaos behind the bars... and just the smell that was coming out of the Dome...and it was the fear of being alone, not knowing at this point what had happened to my family.

I befriended a National Guard and actually slept close to their sleeping quarters to feel safe. I befriended another gentleman and we slept in shifts to watch each other's belongings. Because in the event you were to go to sleep, someone would just walk up and take your things.

There were several rumors circulating in reference to murders and rapes, but I can tell you first hand that on the first day a ten-year-old girl was raped and killed and found in a bathroom. And from that point on, crime just escalated. The National Guard had no control. I mean how can you control 60,000 people, when you only have 300 to 400 National Guards? You're talking about murderers and drug dealers and drug addicts and rapists among a group of normal civilized people. They were just a small percentage, but they caused major chaos for everybody else.

DAVE EICHLER: What really worries me is that the news is just skewing the facts and the figures as best they can, and you know now there's a big push to try to play down the rapes and the murders in the Dome. I mean, there's living proof. They're 60,000 people in there, do you really think that you're going to be able to spread a lie like this and say this never happened? They're saying there's no real proof of any of this. Well, of course there's no real proof. There was no one to report it to. You got 300 National Guard watching 60,000 people and no ammunition in their guns.

ELLEN LYTLE: And no right and no authority to arrest or seize.

DAVE: There was no one to report it to.

MELANIE: On Thursday morning, at 5 a.m., a soldier tapped me on my leg and informed me that the National Guard have an order to pull out because the generators were about to run out of fuel. And if the generators went out, it would just be mad chaos. I guess somebody thought that their safety was more important than ours. I began to cry at that moment. The soldier apologized to me and gave me his knife. He told me the best thing I could do is find somewhere to hide it until active duty could get there, which would take about another two to three days.

And I said, "How could y'all leave us? They're gonna kill us in here. Please don't leave us." Well, luckily the generators didn't go out.

ELLEN: That soldier called later to check on her when she was here.

MELANIE: He did. You know, it's ironic. I actually know a lot about the Superdome because my mom was a tour guide there for twenty-six years. She had just retired from the Dome, so I knew the ins and outs, the hallways, the ramps, the back alleyways. The National Guardsman told me, "If we got to pull out, we're gonna go to Gate A." He said, "I can't say you can come with us, but I can't stop you from running behind us, so if you can haul ass and make it to Gate A, you might be able to get out." I'm like, "I'm going to hold onto the helicopter leg—I'll do whatever I got to do. Y'all are not gonna leave me in this Dome to die with these people." I didn't come to the Superdome to die.

But the generators didn't go out and we couldn't leave. We couldn't leave the Dome. And I think that's what caused a lot of problems. Because there were people who wanted to leave, becoming very loud and angry and pushing barricades, because there were barricades in place so that you could not exit out of certain doors.

ELLEN: They locked them in.

MELANIE: The National Guard was posted with their M16s. And then barricades were placed. So at that point, people just wanted to leave. We had been in there for so long, the food and water was scarce because as trucks were coming in, you had looters who would take over these trucks, taking the water and selling the water for two dollars a bottle, and taking the MREs, the Military Ready-to-Eats. So it's not like there was a system, get in line and you can get your food, or order of any kind.

Where I was, someone would pass by with a box of food and as a family, take an entire box. So you just have to wait until the next round comes around. You had to be vigilant when it came down to just trying to eat and drink. The bathrooms were not in existence then. You used the bathroom publicly. I had to use the bathroom publicly. And the water...look, I knew, just from being in the medical field, not to drink the water. But I did brush my teeth with the water on the first day. There was running water on the first floor of the Dome on Tuesday. I can remember seeing people filling up bottles with water and I'm saying, y'all, please don't drink that water. I'm like, why isn't the National Guard telling the people, "Don't drink the water?" The water is contaminated. But we were not informed. Why didn't they put signs up?

I mean, what was the purpose of the National Guard? Were they medics basically, just to take care of the sick and the elderly? But not to inform, protect or any of those things? I don't know. They said they were powerless.

ELLEN: She brushed her teeth just that one time, and then she was sick for a day and a half.

MELANIE: I caught that mass virus that was going around, with the vomits and diarrhea, just from brushing my teeth with that water. I went to the medical clinic to get some type of IV fluid or something, some Imodium to stop the vomiting and the diarrhea. But they had closed down because there were just too many patients and they had run out of supplies. So I just dealt with it and used the bathroom outside.

They had been announcing all week, "The buses are on their way; the buses are gonna be here." And we're constantly looking around, hoping for those buses. Finally on Friday, they told us to start lining up—it was somewhere about 8 a.m.—and the buses would be here. So of course, it turned into a riot. You can't tell a bunch of people who been locked up and literally in a cage for that long, "Okay, now the buses are here, but we only want to take women and children and elderly first. And we want you all to line up quietly and peaceful." It's not gonna work. So that turned into a riot. It was a horrible experience just trying to actually get on the bus.

The National Guard had assigned me an elderly woman from a nursing home who had Alzheimer's. So that's how I ended up getting on the bus in one of the first loads, because I had a senior citizen with me. I believe that's how a lot of families got separated, because people started grabbing other people's children or grabbing someone elderly just so they could say "Hey, I need to get on this bus first."

They transported us to Houston, and the Houston Police Department came on the bus and told us we could not get off. They reported that rapes and lootings and riots had begun in the Astrodome as well.

So at that point I don't want to go to Houston Astrodome. I don't want to go through this all over again. I felt like God brought me through the storm but when I got to the Superdome I felt like I was left there to die. You know, that was one of the worst experiences. I was sitting in the seats on Wednesday in the Dome when the National Guard had gotten shot. And he couldn't even return fire because his weapon wasn't loaded. It took another National Guardsman to return fire and kill this person in front of thousands of people in the middle of the football field. And I was there when that happened. Sitting in the seats.

It makes you wonder: how did someone get in there with a weapon, when we were searched when we were first brought into the Superdome? Any type of glass items, if we had razors or anything, they took it out of your bags. I even had a rattail comb, they broke the tip off because that could have been used for a weapon.

So it was pretty scary just to think, well, how did these people even get in with weapons or drugs for that matter? They did enforce rules at first, you know, no cigarette smoking, no drug use, but after so long...

DAVE: How about the hot dog stand?

MELANIE: Yeah, there was a hot dog stand set up on the Plaza Level, where they were selling drugs from that hot dog stand. But you know, how could you stop someone from doing these things if you don't have the authority to do it?

In any case, I was *not* going to go to the Houston Astrodome. So I just began walking down the Houston highway. There were a group of men in a truck who were giving out water and juices and crackers. I basically walked up to them. I was crying, distraught, confused, lost, and I just asked them if I could use a cell phone. And they said, "Where are you trying to go to?" I was just trying to call someone from my family, to hear a voice, to see if they were alive because I haven't heard from anyone. So they offered to bring me to the Greyhound bus station and buy me a ticket to wherever I was going.

I told them I had a cousin in Baton Rouge that I needed to get to Baton Rouge. But unfortunately, the buses only brought me to Lake Charles, Louisiana. So from Lake Charles to Baton Rouge, I hitchhiked a ride. I stayed in Baton Rouge two days at my cousin's apartment. But after two days, I didn't want to be in Baton Rouge. I didn't feel safe there. Curfews were being enforced because crime instantly went up. I tried the Red Cross Shelter there but it was overwhelmed with people.

So from there I went to Hammond, Louisiana, to a girlfriend of mine. Unfortunately in Hammond, FEMA had not arrived there yet, so getting aid or assistance wasn't good. So they brought me to Amite, Louisiana, where I was able to apply for food stamps. And that took a forty-eight-hour process.

While I was in Hammond, I went on the Internet and just typed in "hurricane housing." Because at this point, I'm homeless. I don't have any food. I don't have any shelter. I just need to get somewhere. I didn't feel safe in Louisiana at all, didn't feel safe nowhere. And I submitted an application, told them about myself, my situation. There were ads set up saying what someone had to offer. Ellen responded by calling me.

ELLEN: I get a weekly email from MoveOn.org. They sent an email about HurricaneHousing. It was just a general call, "Does anybody want to help?" Giving money to Red Cross is wonderful, but it's detached, it's not an act of participation. I'm a college professor. I teach graphic design. I have a teaching salary so I don't have that much money. But I have an extra room and an extra bath and if I could just help one person that would be doing something a little more personal than just sending a check to an anonymous organization.

It was just gut reaction. Like, "I can do this." And I remember at the same time, I was watching the news, just dumbfounded. Watching the government fly over the top of this tragedy and nobody going down to see what was going on. It made me genuinely angry, and it was aggravating to just sit, stand by and see nothing happen. It was like the whole system was falling apart right in front of us.

So I put an ad up and said, "I am in Marietta, we have bus service, live two blocks from the bus line, and I can take a mother and child or two children or single person." I posted, and Melanie responded to a couple of them, and I responded back first. And I think you found out there were good jobs in Marietta, so that sounded like a good place to go?

MELANIE: Yeah. Because I had a normal life before the storm. I was career-oriented, so just to wake up and not have everything that you once had is something that you just can't imagine. You go to sleep one night and you wake up the next morning and it's all gone. And it's no going back. No going back at all.

ELLEN: We crossed phone calls for at least a day or so. It's because the cell phones, the towers and stuff, were down all over Louisiana.

You can tell a lot about a person talking to them for a couple minutes. And Melanie wrote very clearly in her note, "I wish someone would please help me." Just very honest about asking for help. People usually only do that they're seriously in trouble.

I can never stand by and let bad things happen to other people. (*Laughs*) Yeah, it's got me into trouble in the past. Funny way to live your life. Sometimes it has repercussions.

But I could just tell from talking to her that she was ready to start over. She was just very clear about what she needed to do. She had a plan. She wasn't lost other than what had happened to her.

MELANIE: So we met up in Livingston, Alabama. We met a gas station.

DAVE: I went and helped with the driving. I am my sister's brother, so I'm a chronic do-gooder as well. So when she said, "Let's go, we're leaving tomorrow morning," I just said, "Okay. I'll be there." So we loaded up the car and drove out and picked her up.

ELLEN: She didn't have anything but just one little bag, one that her friend had given her, so there wasn't much to pick up.

She told us the stories on the way there, and we were both shocked at how dramatic they were compared to what we had been hearing on the news. And she was so exhausted. She was telling us what was going on and just right in the middle of a sentence she just fell asleep. And David and I looked at each other and thought, *oh my God.* Because it was ten times worse than anything we saw on the news. And I'm sure she didn't even have the worst experience.

I put boxes of Kleenex all over the apartment so she could just grab a Kleenex if she got upset. She was so numb. I said, "If it was me, first thing I'd want to do is sit down and have a good cry." And she said, "I've been crying for two weeks. I'm completely numb." She only cried one time. So I'm thinking, *It's going to catch up with her later and the whole thing is just gonna come down on her.*

MELANIE: It was comforting. But at the same time it still felt so empty, because I didn't know at that point where my mom was, my aunts, my cousins or anything. I was still presuming that they were all deceased. I went onto the Red Cross registry once I got here, to try to look up family members, but no one's names had been registered. I'm like, "God, it's been two weeks—how do I know they're still alive? What do I do?" And as much as Ellen tried to make me comfortable, there were nights when I still cried in my room. But I knew from this point on I had to do something for myself, because I had not received any assistance except for food stamps, which is limited. And I was getting the run-around from FEMA, Red Cross. The 1-800 number practically just didn't work. I thought it was a bogus number.

ELLEN: It kept saying, "This is a non-working number." The number that they put on television that said, "Call here"? Well, it was not a working number.

MELANIE: I remember when we first got here, Ellen offered to take me swimming. I said, "Oh, *no.*" I didn't realize I had a phobia with water. It took me maybe two weeks or more to take a full bath.

ELLEN: She wouldn't take a full bath or a shower.

MELANIE: Water to my ankles.

ELLEN: She didn't want the shower water hitting her face. She was terrified of water running on her face. She said, "I'm just going to take a bath in an inch of water."

MELANIE: I talked to my mother two weeks ago for the first time. She had been transported to a shelter in Arkansas.

They had been rescued! Yes, all are accounted for. We are just very spread out right now. My daughters are with their dad in Columbus, Mississippi. We thought that was best for them, since he's a school teacher and was able to find work, and his wife is a nurse. His life has changed too. He had his own brass jazz band and his way of life is totally altered. But I need to get my girls back to be with me. I miss them.

I'm still not comfortable with being here. There's never gonna be a place like home, you know. Just the whole concept of this happening is unimaginable to me. The whole lifestyle is different here. It's basically a culture shock. New Orleans was known for its jazz, its music, its love of fun. It was a close-knit family and community. Here it's very multicultural and it's just hard getting to know people and trying to figure out your way around town.

Ellen is definitely my support system here. Through Ellen, I do have an extended family now, her friends and family.

ELLEN: I put out an email to everybody who I knew was of a like mind, and said, "All points bulletin, here's what's going on. Here's what Melanie needs." Everybody just responded back with emails and I got two suits in a size-twelve she can wear on interviews. And I called all my friends and made them give me Target gift certificates and we're going to take her shopping. But it took a lot of people to just take care of one person. It's so oversimplified that you can give someone a couple of food stamps and then they should be okay now.

MELANIE: I've sent out over fifty applications. I was a dental assistant in New Orleans. I have experience. But I didn't even hear back. Why don't they hire us? I think they are afraid we'll go back to New Orleans or we're stigmatized as criminals.

I'm not going back to New Orleans. Where I lived, it's not even a living area anymore. We paid $475 a month for a two-bedroom and now it's a thousand a month. So I can't go back. It was a low-income city and the landlords are doubling the rent. The mayor said legally they aren't breaking any laws, so they can't stop it. And I wonder about everyone from back home. Did they make it? There were so many elderly there. Where are they now?

So I can't go back. Right now I'm staying in an apartment through the Red Cross

I still haven't gotten any assistance from FEMA. I sent them a copy of my lease and I turned in my application on September 7th. Still nothing. They just want us to go away. If I hadn't heard of MoveOn.org, I don't know where I'd be.

I'm okay though. I've been writing songs. I'm a spoken word artist. I write poetry, try to get my thoughts out, you know. My friend and I, we put a microphone in the bathroom and record songs.

ELLEN: I told her, "You can stay here with me for months." I know she feels like she's imposing. She is not used to not having anything and having people say, "Here have some money, here have this, have that." I can see it in her face; she's very uncomfortable. It's like taking charity or something for the first time in your life. It's demeaning and demoralizing to be put in that position and she's not that kind of person. I don't blame her for being uncomfortable.

MELANIE: It's true. But once we connected, it did give me a more positive outlook. I just didn't feel safe, and through HurricaneHousing I was able to stay in a safe place and at least get a new lease on life and start over. Even though it may seem like I still don't have so many things, I'm grateful for what I do have. It's just good to know that if I do fall short, I have someone to call. Because right now my family is in the same boat that I am in. We're all still waiting on some type of public assistance and we can't rely on each other. We can't hold each other up right now. So it's the help of other people, privately, who are really making a difference.

ELLEN: I like the company. I'm perfectly happy to have her stay here forever.

MELANIE: She teaches me different things about the city, you know, landmarks and kudzu, which is that…

ELLEN: Kudzu, that creature plant that eats…

MELANIE: Creature plants, they eat everything up.

ELLEN: What sweet tea is…

MELANIE: They're serious about sweet tea out here. I mean, you order tea at a restaurant, sweet or unsweet? How sweet do you want it, you know? It's just small things I miss, like, going to the grocery store and asking for red beans and ham, things that we ordinarily have in New Orleans.

Although Katrina has devastated many of our lives, at least mine, it has given me a fresh start, to start over again. And hopefully this time, the second time around it'll be better.

I don't have anything to return to. I lived in the little Ninth Ward and once Rita came, the levee broke and it re-flooded the area where I once lived. So I don't have a home to go back to.

I'm going to stay in Georgia. Just where I don't know. I like Georgia, but I don't know exactly where I'm going to stay.

Ellen says, "Stay with me, stay with me." But I was independent before. I have goals I have to meet and I have two little girls. They're worried. They say, "Mom, do you have food?"

FEMA said, "We'll assign you a trailer." But I say, "Where will I put it?" I don't have any land. They say, "We'll send you to where one is." But those trailers aren't in industrial areas. They're in rural areas and there are no jobs there. So okay, y'all sign me up for it but if my number comes up, I don't have anywhere to put a trailer. And a trailer? I don't want to be blown away after what I've been through. Sometimes I think I don't want to be anywhere on the Gulf Coast.

Nothing can be worse then waking up and everything you have is gone. Only thing worse would be dying but at least then you'd be in heaven.

ELLEN: You know that phrase, "It takes a village"? It's gonna take a village for each person to fix this. It's gonna take a whole group of people just to put one person back together.

DAVE: It's gonna take the whole country to put this whole thing back together. ↪

"BUT YOU DON'T HAVE TO WORRY, ROZ. I'm here."

ROZ DANIELS: I was living in Arabi, Louisiana, just over the Orleans Parish line, in St. Bernard Parish. Which was one of the hardest hit parishes. I lived alone. I was working at the time as a home health caregiver. And my daughter lived in Meraux, so unfortunately when the Industrial Canal broke, it not only flooded my home but hers.

We evacuated on Saturday, two days before Katrina hit on Monday. It was me, my daughter, my son-in-law and my two granddaughters. We drove straight to Marietta, Georgia.

My daughter and her family were put up by their company in a Marietta hotel. The accommodations were very, very small—basically a bare room with a couple of double beds. There was just no way I could stay with them. Luckily, my daughter found Carlotta online on Hurricane-Housing.org.

CARLOTTA ROBERTS: We met them for lunch on a Saturday afternoon. I really wanted to help in some way and this seemed like a good person to take. Roz and I are about the same age so we knew we'd get along okay, right? (*Laughs*) My husband and I have had people live with us on and off for about thirty years. We've taken lots of people in. Now, no one quite as nice as Roz! (*Laughter*)

But, yeah, we've had lots of people live with us so it's never a problem. And we have plenty of room. You know, it's just the two of us, my husband and me. And with Roz needing surgery and all, it just seemed natural to help her.

ROZ: I had been told before the hurricane that I needed open heart surgery. But the hurricane messed up my operation plans. So when we arrived I knew that it was critical that I get the surgery taken care of right away. I was recommended to a surgeon from Kennesaw. And they immediately took me in and performed the surgery. I've been here in Marietta about three weeks total now, and have been recovering at Carlotta's house for about eight days.

CARLOTTA: Mmhmm, you've been here about a total three weeks.

ROZ: Just got out of the hospital eight days ago. I still have a forty-five-week recovery ahead of me.

Carlotta giving me a place to stay and a safe place to recover from my surgery—well it has really been a lifesaver, a Godsend, you might say. We were holding onto a small amount of hope that we might be able to salvage something and go back home. But after hearing the reports on Monday, we pretty much knew we wouldn't be ...oh...(*starts sobbing*)...no, don't let me cry...

CARLOTTA: Come on now.

ROZ: We knew we wouldn't be going back. There's no going back. (*Cries*)

CARLOTTA: Roz...

ROZ: I have nothing. My house is gone, all my possessions, our vehicles, my job, my friends, my neighbors, all in one day. My little girl, her house is gone, destroyed. Within a day all of her friends were scattered. You just can't imagine what it's like. Trying to find out if people you know and love are alive, trying to find out if your neighbors got out okay—friends and neighbors that I'd had for fifteen years. We're all just frantically trying to find each other. Just trying to figure out what's going on.

CARLOTTA: Tell them the good piece of news that you had today.

ROZ: Oh, I found my cat! (*Laughs*) I found my cat. They allowed some of the residents of St. Bernard Parish to go back in and see if there was anything left to recover. So my son-in-law went back and they had found my cat! He was just sitting at home, waiting to be rescued. (*Laughs*)

I'm sorry. I hate it when I start to cry. I've almost gotten over that though.

[left to right] Carlotta Roberts (host), Roslyn Daniels (evacuee)

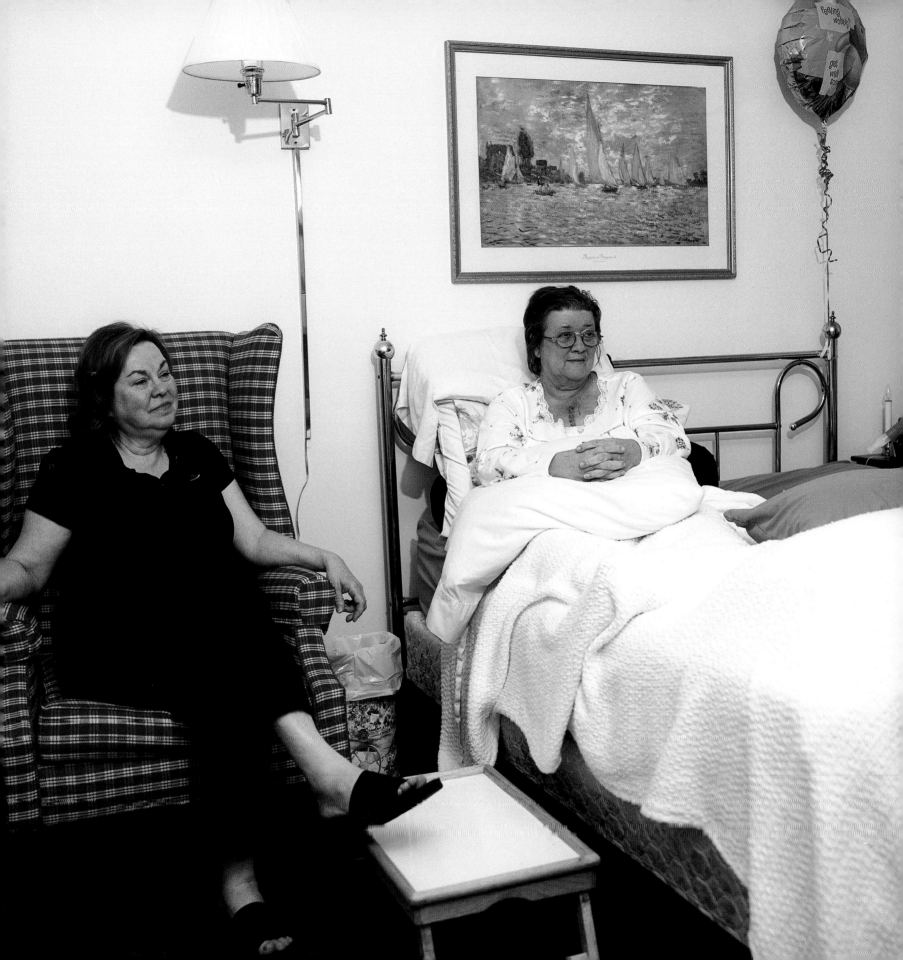

CARLOTTA: I think you're doing really well.

ROZ: I've cried every day for the past month but now I'm getting better.

CARLOTTA: It's good to cry, I think.

ROZ: Yeah, I think it helps a little.

CARLOTTA: Well, you know, major surgery kind of plays with your emotions too, Roz! *(Laughter)*

ROZ: Yes, I suppose it does. I want to say that everyone here has been wonderful, absolutely wonderful to me. I came here as a refugee. Yes, that's what they call us because that's what we are. We got the clothes on our back and beyond that we've got nothing. And everyone has been just so patient. Everyone has just gone out of their way for me. Everybody at the hospital was so great and took such good care of me. They even transferred my insurance just like that without question.

And Carlotta has been an angel, visiting me all the time and letting me stay here. We get along great.

CARLOTTA: Yeah, we get along great.

ROZ: She's wonderful.

CARLOTTA: And we're very close in age.

ROZ: Well…

CARLOTTA: OK, I'm a little older, but not much! *(Laughter)*

ROZ: You cannot imagine how much harder it would be on me and my family if I couldn't stay here. If Carlotta wasn't taking such good care of me.

CARLOTTA: And people from our church are helping too. I have to go back to work this week and I don't want her left here alone. She's just back from the hospital and she needs looking after, so friends of mine from church are gonna sit with her this week and make sure she's okay. They'll just sit with her while I'm at the office.

ROZ: If Carlotta weren't here, helping me like this…well, I don't know what I would do. My daughter and son-in-law have to work every day. They have two daughters and they've lost everything as well. If they had to look after me on top of all that…well, it would be very, very bad. Much harder on them and me.

CARLOTTA: That's for sure. But you don't have to worry, Roz. I'm here. ⇨

ANAIZ STINSON: You know, there was nothing significant about her posting. It was just a one-line little blip that said "house in Kennesaw, cul-de-sac." Nothing significant. But for some reason it was the first one that I emailed. While I was looking through other postings, Tess called me. It was just the way she was—her whole demeanor on the phone.

I told her our basic information and she just sounded so damn cheerful! *(Laughs)* I mean, she just sounded like someone I would want to get to know. She sounded like someone I would want my daughter and myself to live with. ↩

[back row, left to right] Anaiz Stinson (evacuee), Tawn Wooten (host);
[front row, left to right] Carina Stinson (evacuee's daughter), Jada Wooten (host's daughter),
Tess Wooten (host), Lauren Newby (host's daughter)

"IT'S A CHANGE. BECAUSE BASICALLY we come from the city—you know, the high crime rate. I mean, I used to go to bed hearing gunshots at night. That was my lullaby, gunshots at night in New Orleans. I haven't heard that since I've been here."

JARRAUD ANDREWS: All right. Well, I lived at 2010 Touro in New Orleans, Louisiana, which is the Seventh Ward. I grew up in New Orleans. I was a cook and a dishwasher.

EARL DENNIS LANG: I'm also from New Orleans. I used to be in Seventh Ward for four years. But I was in the Ninth Ward when the flood happened: 2017 Alva.

I was self-employed. Mostly I worked for a man named Jerry, doin' all sortsa odd jobs. Jerry had lots of different businesses.

JARRAUD: When the hurricane hit, there were reports that they would be sheltering people at the Convention Center and at the Superdome. Well, me and my parents, we didn't wanna go there. My mother decided she wanted us to wait it out at home. Because at the Convention Center or Superdome, you wouldn't have any food. Not a whole lot of food. Not a whole lot of water. And we had enough supplies in the house to last us two or three weeks.

Still, we had all agreed that if things were still bad after one week, we would leave. Because my mother and my father can't be in that kind of situation. I'm a young man, so I could have handled it. But they needed to get somewhere safe. So Sunday, a week after the hurricane first hit, we all made our way to the Convention Center. We got a ride there in a bus. And at the Convention Center, they put us on an Army helicopter.

We waited for a minute while they checked our bags to make sure we didn't have any weapons or anything like that. And then we were on that helicopter. It was only about five minutes between getting off of the bus before we were on that helicopter.

They didn't exactly tell us where we were headed. They just said we were gonna go somewhere. So they took us to a military base. And from there they put me and my parents, along with maybe about fifty or sixty other people, on a plane to Atlanta. But we didn't go directly to Atlanta. First they took us to the Rock Eagle 4-H Center at Eatonton, Georgia. We stayed there for about two weeks, getting paperwork things out of the way, getting a few clothes, the necessities that we were gonna need. And then that's when we met with Miss Susan. Miss Susan Wilson.

SUSAN WILSON: That's me! *(Laughter)* I met both Jarraud and Earl at the same time. Earl, you had a pretty wild time too, before you got here. ...

EARL: That's true. Well, the day the hurricane hit, I woke up in the morning, I don't know, about eight or nine. And the floodwaters, they wasn't but at the second step of my house. And as time passed, it got up to about five steps to the house. The wind was blowing kind of hard. And, like, about every ten minutes, the water was going up a step. Well, luckily for me, it stopped there. The water stopped right before it got above my front steps! I honestly thought it was gonna swallow my whole house.

Anyhow, the next day, the water was going down slow. And I seen a dude walking past my house. And a while later, he came back driving a city bus. And I said, "You work on the bus? You a city bus driver?" And he said, "No. There are a bunch of buses down the way at the transit yard. You can get one too. Just make sure you know how to operate it."

[left to right] Jarraud Andrews (evacuee), James Wilson (host), Susan Wilson (host), Earl Dennis Lang (evacuee), (front) Jonathan Wilson (host's son)

SUSAN: These are city transit buses just sitting there, down the street from where Earl lived. Two hundred of them were sitting there.

EARL: So me and my buddy Joe went down there. And we ain't got no keys for these buses. But there was some dude walkin' around the bus yard. And he was like, "Go choose a bus. They got somebody back there will show you how to start 'em." And somebody was back there. He showed us how to turn the engine on and cut the button. Got to make sure it's in neutral and then press this black button. You got to get to 150 pressure. Ain't gonna move 'til it get to 150. Pressure's got to go up. Once you get that, just press the button and the bus starts.

So in other words, me and Joe got that bus. And we started drivin', with the thought in mind that we were gonna help people. Then we saw a cop coming behind us. It was a captain. And we said, "We're driving around helping people." And he said, "No. Show *me* how to start the bus. I'm gonna take this here bus. You can go ahead and get another bus, but don't drive it through no high water." He said it was all right that we took that bus 'cause it was a "Code 7." That's what he told me. All right.

So I showed him how to start it and he took it. And we went to get another bus. *(Laughter)* Yeah. Me and Joe and another dude. We went and got another one. And we drove around for a while. And the police, they took that one too. I'm trying to think of when they took that bus. It's hard to remember because we ended up having four buses in front of our door by the end of the day. *(Laughter)*

I give two or three buses away. That's what I'm gonna say to that.

Yeah. But the last time the cops got me, they pulled out guns on me.

SUSAN: The fourth time.

EARL: The fourth. And I showed them how to start the bus. And the police took the bus. But before that I helped quite a few people. We took people to the evacuation site. We had about fifteen or twenty people on the bus at a time.

SUSAN: They'd stop 'em and pick 'em up.

EARL: And we take 'em back to this school where people were evacuatin' to. Well, the last time we went there, the National Guard had about six or seven dudes waiting for us. And they said, "You, you, you the one taking the buses?" I said, "Well, this police captain said this was a 'Code 7'—he told me I could use the buses to help people." You know? And the National Guard said, "Well, I don't want you to take no more buses. If anybody drives a bus, you're gonna go to jail." That's what he told us. So I walked away.

I told Joe, "We ain't taking no more buses. We'll just use the ones we got in front of the door at night with the air condition on." So we left 'em parked in front of the house with the air condition running, and people would come in and sleep in 'em.

SUSAN: Because it was hot as all get-out.

EARL: Yeah. And then that Sunday, a week after the hurricane, I just decided to leave, all by myself. I ended up catching a bus by City Hall. And they brought us to the airport, put us on a plane and said, "Y'all going to Atlanta."

And when I got there they brought me to what was—I think it was the Wildlife Building at the 4-H. And I seen Miss Wilson's name on a list. They said, "She'll help you. Go in the morning. She'll take you in the morning and help you find a job." And I thought, "Well that's better than me going to a shelter. At least I got a head start." You know? So I called 'em.

SUSAN: We live in Athens, Georgia. I work at the University of Georgia in the Textile Science department. I'm a lab coordinator. And my husband is a surveyor.

I get emails from MoveOn all the time, and I got one right after the hurricane hit about HurricaneHousing.org. So I signed up for it. And some volunteers from the University printed out the listing and distributed the postings at 4-H. That's what Earl saw. He called me on Saturday, and we went to pick him up on Sunday. We only thought we were getting Earl. And then while we were on the way, they called us again and said, "Hey, we have another guy. Will you take him too?" And I was like, "Sure." And that was Jarraud.

JARRAUD: Yeah. I had went to the wildlife building that day to just see if I could find a place to go to. And a young lady asked me if I wanted to go with Earl. And I was like, "Of course I'm willing to go. But you know we have to be able to give these people a little bit of time to get things straight." I wanted to find out first if it was okay. You can't just say, "Well yeah, I'm gonna go." I wasn't sure if they would be willing to accept me too.

SUSAN: It's been no problem. They've been really great guys. The first thing up, they said they wanted a job. And the day after they got here, we went to the University of Georgia human resources. And they got Earl and Jarraud jobs on the grounds.

JARRAUD: I started working at the UG Monday.

SUSAN: Monday. Yeah.

JARRAUD: We both got jobs at the Physical Plant department. We're both groundskeepers. It's been pretty good. Pretty good. I mean I've done that kind of work when I was in New Orleans—landscaping and whatnot. So I'm getting paid to do something I actually enjoy doing, which is always a plus. And the pay is way better. I'm making like almost three dollars more than I was in New Orleans.

EARL: Uh-huh. I'm satisfied.

JIM WILSON: I was glad to help them too. You know what I mean?

SUSAN: Jim knows I do things like this all the time.

(Laughter)

JM: Yeah. She likes to help people as much as she can.

SUSAN: I mean, I could not imagine myself being in the same situation, and having no family, no support. No way to find a job, having your entire life absolutely flooded. If I was in that situation, I'd really hope someone would be there to help me. I mean, I grew up in South Africa. So I have seen real poverty firsthand.

My family ended up in Georgia because my dad was really anti-apartheid. He was getting in trouble for speaking out against it. And so we left. He was a professor and got a job here at the University of Georgia. I was fifteen.

I didn't like milk when I was a kid. And my parents used to make me drink my milk, and made me feel guilty about not wanting to drink it, because there were people all around us in South Africa who had no milk to drink. And I thought if I ever got the money, I'd just like to buy milk for all the children who don't have any. I've just always had a real soft spot for people who are in a tough situation.

So helping these two has been a little bit of work, but now we've got 'em set up. They've got everything now. They've got TV. They've got beds. They've got everything. They actually moved out of our place yesterday.

JARRAUD: We're staying at University Gardens.

SUSAN: A garden apartment.

JARRAUD: He has his own apartment. I have my own.

SUSAN: Well, I called around.

EARL: She did a lot of work. A lot of work. She helped us out a lot.

SUSAN: Yeah. I had to do a lot of wheeling and dealing. For instance, the power company tried to charge them some outrageous deposit. And I ended up getting them to charge nothing—no deposit. I had to do the whole "who's your supervisor?" kind of thing. And then I got these guys set up with some food donations. Because they don't get paid for three weeks basically. Their jobs started in on the middle of a pay period. And they only get paid every two weeks.

But I mean you're pretty well-shacked up now, aren't you guys?

JARRAUD: We're good to go. We're on a six-month lease right now. And FEMA is paying for our first six months of rent. FEMA's been pretty good, they've given us the assistance that we've needed. But mostly it's Susan, she's just helped us so much.

Now I'm just excited to be here. I'm ready to just do whatever. I can fit in anywhere. I can fit in anywhere in the country. And I feel like this is a great chance for me to do what I needed to do that I couldn't do in New Orleans—like get my life right.

SUSAN: What these guys are doing now, here in Georgia, would have been a minimum wage job in New Orleans. And they would have been lucky to get it. Because unemployment was extremely high. And the crime rate was extremely high. New Orleans has one of the largest murder rates in the U.S.

So, I mean, we got them jobs that are a lot better pay than it would have been in New Orleans. And better benefits. And a nice, kind of quiet place to live.

EARL: I feel good.

JARRAUD: It's a change. Because basically we come from the city—you know, the high crime rate. I mean, I used to go to bed hearing gunshots at night. That was my lullaby—gunshots at night in New Orleans. I haven't heard that since I've been here. And I'm loving it. Because, you know, it's a totally different place.

I wasn't doing well in New Orleans, you know? There was just too much stuff, too much aggravation. Too much stress. Too much pressure to try to do the right things. And it was so easy to do the wrong things to make money. I'd rather make it the hard way and honestly than to be out there and make it the easy way. In New Orleans, the only way to make good money is to do it the easy way. And the easy way is just to be illegal. And I'm not gonna do that. Because my record is clean and I aim to keep it that way. I'm fine. I ain't trying to go that route.

EARL: I'm gonna go back and visit New Orleans at Christmas. But I don't think I'm gonna go back to stay. I don't know. I don't see that. I doubt it.

SUSAN: Never say never.

JARRAUD: Well, I'm just lookin' forward to gettin' to know this place better. And makin' some new friends. I've already met a few neighbors around this area by the Wilsons. In New Orleans, you could walk outside your door and see everybody just hanging out. Here, it's quiet. Everybody kind of stays to themselves, but they still know each other. I mean, I've made a few friends. People I can talk to or hang out with sometimes. People that can help me, show me around the city, teach me about some things that go on in Georgia and in Athens. Yeah. I've already made a few good friends.

EARL: I got two dudes that I work with that I get along with.

SUSAN: They wanted to go fishing and to the flea market. But he was moving this weekend, so he couldn't go.

EARL: Yeah. I don't know. Maybe next weekend.

SUSAN: You should go then.

EARL: You know, I think I will. ⇨

FEMA Urban Search and Rescue team members searching for residents in New Orleans.

"GOD SENT PEOPLE WHO HAD A LOT of love in their hearts for giving, and weren't looking for the receiving of anything. It was heart warming and heart touching. You could just feel the invitation of the whole thing, when it happened."

RONALD ANDREWS: We lived in the eastern part of New Orleans and it was hit the hardest. We were really affected, as far as property damage.

The day before, everybody was talking about, should we leave? I was on the phone with my brothers and my sisters. I said, "I don't know. I never ran from a hurricane, my grandmother never ran from a hurricane." I decided just to pray on it, and after I went to sleep that night, God gave me my answer. That morning, I told them, "We going. We booking out."

We just jumped up and gathered some things together and headed on out. Me and my girls, Shadika, Ashley, Latoya, Wendy and even grandbaby Alia, and my mother and my grandmother. There were fifteen of us all together. We had four cars and we loaded up and headed toward Alabama, trying to get hotels along the way, but we couldn't find nothing nowhere. So I said "Let's keep on rolling."

Once we hit the Georgia state line, the closest place was Marietta. We stayed at the Super 8 in Marietta for maybe about a week. Some of the family members got real disgusted with it. We lost my brother and his family. They decided to go back. But my niece had a laptop and my brother used it and went online and found Connie's ad, offering assistance. They came and found us. God brought us here to them so we could get stable.

CONNIE TUCKER: After the hurricane happened, everybody was fussing and complaining about the slow response of the government. It just got to a point where complaining wasn't gonna do anything, you know? So I'm thinking, *I'd love to help a family out, but I'm afraid to say something to my husband.* Because we're not financially rich. We both work every single day. I work for Cingular Wireless. I'm a data specialist. My husband Chris has his own courier business, but he's the owner and the only employee.

I called several radio stations and shelters. I called the Red Cross and the Salvation Army. No one could set us up with a family. They basically said, "We don't do that." Then one day my husband sent me a text message that said, "How do you feel about sponsoring a family?"

It was like God answered my prayers, because I was waiting for him to say it. We had put this house on the market because we just purchased another home about thirty minutes further east, so it was actually perfect timing. Ten minutes after my husband sent me the text message, my girlfriend sent out an email that said anyone who wanted to help evacuees, here's a website—MoveOn.org. I went online and I posted, saying we had a four-bedroom house with three-and-a-half bathrooms. It was definitely enough house.

God had this all planned out. He had a script, and it was just up to us to follow the script. One of my co-workers lives out by Six Flags and she said a lot of people were living out there in their cars. So that Friday night, my husband said, "Let's ride out to the parking lot at Six Flags—we're gonna look for a family." We'd just gotten on Interstate 85 when Roger called. I said, "How many are there?" And Roger said, "It's a lot of us." He wouldn't give me an exact number. (*Laughter*)

But there was something about his voice. I started snapping my fingers, telling my husband, "Turn around.

[back row, left to right] Ronald Andrews (evacuee), Mary Tureaud (evacuee), Robin Kelley Sarapo (evacuee), Connie Tucker (host); [third row, left to right] Latonia Collins (evacuee), Shade Collins (evacuee), Roger Kelley (evacuee), Ashley Andrews (evacuee); [second row, left to right] Nadia Summers (evacuee), Anya Summers (evacuee), Trina Mack (evacuee); [front row, left to right] Alia Mack (evacuee), Roderick Kelley (evacuee), Larry Kelley (evacuee), Jimmie Kelley (evacuee)

We got our family." I asked Roger, "Where are you guys at now?" He said, "The Super 8 in Marietta." Chris said, "Well, we're gonna go and meet them. Let's go."

We didn't meet all fifteen of them right away. I met Robin, Roger and Ron. I saw a few of the teenagers, maybe one or two of the kids, but not everybody. I told my husband, "God be moving things," because we posted for a family of eight. I thought, *Wow, God gave me fifteen, and he gave me both older people and kids*. I just felt like we were so blessed to be able to do this.

Roger said that they figured they'd be gone for two or three days, so that's all they brought with them, and they were running out of money. We told them what we were trying to do—we let them know we're not rich people but that something moved us in our hearts to do this and we wanted to help them as much as we could. Then we started scouring up friends and co-workers, saying, "Okay, what can you do? What can you give? We need this, we need that." Everybody pitched in.

ROBIN SARAPO: The very next day, the house was furnished, and I mean, anything you'd need when you move into a house. Connie and her husband made it happen for us. Everything. It was amazing.

CONNIE: All the stuff in the house is either loaned or given by friends. If I go back to the hair salon, they're like, "I got some more stuff for you." It's been amazing just to see how people have stepped up to bat. While we were picking up furniture at the Salvation Army, we met a couple who were giving away things, and I said, "Excuse me, but do you have anything else that you want to get rid of? We're trying to help a family out that was affected by the storm." And they were like, "We have a queen-size bed." It was just awesome.

RONALD: Right away, we knew that it was all blessings. I said, "God answered our prayers now and we'll see where we'll go from here." And the amazing part was that when he sent somebody, he didn't just send anybody. He sent people who had a lot of love in their hearts for giving and weren't looking for the receiving of anything. It was heart-warming and heart-touching. You could just feel the invitation of the whole thing, when it happened. I felt relieved. It lifted a lot of stress off us.

ROBIN: We moved in the next day.

CONNIE: We met them over at the house, and they pulled up in about five cars! I got whiplash watching all the cars pull up! I'm thinking, okay, when is this going to stop? (*Laughs*) It was four generations: the great-grandmother, her children, their children, and then one of their kids had a kid. They ranged from eighty-two to two.

MARY TUREAUD: It was a blessing for us to come into a new house where we all were together. There wasn't nothing we could do about our home, what we'd left. But this was nice. We were satisfied. It was a great blessing.

RONALD: When they offered us the house, they weren't looking to get anything back. After we got settled and all, then we started getting some assistance from the government, which was a real help. But from the beginning, if we had not received the love from Connie and Chris, our resources would have *never* lasted until we got assistance from the government. We'd have been stuck somewhere else. There ain't no telling how it may have ended up. We would have probably never reached a point where we got a roof, especially for all of us to be together.

CONNIE: Our real estate agent was pushing for us to go ahead and put the house back on the market, because houses are really selling in the area. We'll just have to hold off on that. We gotta make sure that Ronald and his family are okay. You can't turn your back on people. You just can't. They're helping out a lot with the mortgage, which is around $1,500 a month, but we're still paying part of it. We told them if they want to buy the house, they could just pay off the mortgage, without us making a profit. We made that offer to them.

RONALD: We don't know how long it may last, but right now, we have an agreement with them for three months. From that, we don't know. We'll deal with it as it comes up. I don't know if we're gonna go back to New Orleans. Not to live.

MARY: I will. I will go back. I've lived there ever since I was eighteen years old, and right now I'm eighty-two. They were letting people come back, but not to the area where I was living—out in the east that got hit the worst. So whenever they let me come home, I'll be glad.

RONALD: My thing is, God told Lot to take his family out of there and don't look back. I think Lot's story gave me a perfect example to not to look back, to keep going on. And here in Atlanta, things are starting to fall in place for me. I was a bus operator before. I'm driving school buses here now. You only work five hours a day, but that's better than nothing.

ROBIN: I have to go back and forth to handle business. I have two homes in New Orleans and I have to take care of that. But I work for U.S. Customs, so I can pretty much go anywhere. I'm on administrative leave right now. When I do go back to work, it will be at the Atlanta airport.

ROGER KELLEY: I was a manager at Pizza Hut and an industrial labor worker. A crane operator. I'm not too much looking forward to going back home. I do wanna go back to see the damage that was done to my apartment, but I'm looking for a home out here and work out here.

ROBIN: There's just so much love from the people of Atlanta.

RONALD: Multiple people. Sometimes you may see some help coming from two or three people, but when you get a multiple of people reaching out for you, man, it's real amazing. It's a totally new situation.

SHADIKA ANDREWS: I have new schooling too. Norcross High School. I'm a senior. It's great. You meet new people, learn new things. It's hard at the same time, but I'm dealing with it.

CONNIE: Ronald and his whole family—they were just like us, trying to work every day, make a life, make a home for their families. They just had bad luck. You could tell they weren't used to people coming by and giving, giving, giving.

RONALD: We haven't really had time to just sit down amongst ourselves and think about what we've come from. We've been too busy pressing forward, trying to get something going ahead. But I feel like Connie and her family are part of our family now, too.

ROBIN: Everybody's looking forward to the New Orleans gumbo that I promised. We just have to coordinate a time when we can all get together. I plan on going back next week to New Orleans. I have a pot that I always cook my gumbo in, and I'm gonna get it this time. It's about this tall. I don't know how many gallons are in that pot. Maybe fifty gallons.

RONALD: Yeah, that's a fifty-gallon pot. As a matter of fact, that's my pot I left there. (*Laughter*)

ROBIN: No, it's not yours! I have one—the one I always cook in. Actually, I got it when I was in the military. I used to do a gumbo in Germany, and I always cook gumbo like that for the family. So I'm gonna get it and bring it back here.

RONALD: I hope she can get all the ingredients from there too. Somewhere in Louisiana, we should be able to get it. We miss the food. That and the transportation. The city transit in New Orleans ran in all the neighborhoods, everywhere. You ain't gotta have a car to get around. I know that's been missed, bigtime. And the corner stores, because people in New Orleans love walking to the corner store.

ROBIN: We do have cars, but unfortunately, not everybody, so it's pretty hard. Like for Ashley, this was her first year in college, and she's had to miss her first semester because we just don't have anybody available to make sure that she gets there and back. We're working on getting her a car so she can start the next semester.

ASHLEY ANDREWS: I was going to go to Delgado Community College, before the storm. The schools here were willing to take me in, but now they don't have any openings for me to start, to go towards my major, which is nursing. I have two in mind here—Georgia State and Georgia Perimeter. Maybe in January.

CONNIE: When we met them, Robin kept saying, "Y'all gonna be so blessed." And I'm like, "You know what—we're already blessed. If we hadn't been blessed, we couldn't do this." So that's what you do. You share the blessings. ⇨

MICHELLE PETERSON
DENNIS SCOTT

STONE MOUNTAIN,
GEORGIA

SIERRA MOHAWK
ERAN CASSIDINE

"I HAD NO PROBLEM BRINGING STRANGERS into the house. Whenever you have dinner together, you quit being strangers. Food is a universal thing."

MICHELLE PETERSON: We're all from New Orleans. Just before Katrina hit, I had lost my job.

DENNIS SCOTT: I was working and living in the public housing district.

MICHELLE: First place we went when the hurricane came was the Superdome. We were there, what, about seven days? It wasn't a positive experience. It just was bad, that's all.

DENNIS: Got out by bus—to Oklahoma.

MICHELLE: We were in Oklahoma about two weeks. At a military base.

SIERRA MOHAWK: And when they were at the Dome there was a little girl there who couldn't find her parents. Michelle and Dennis took care of her.

MICHELLE: Her grandmother was afraid of her being in the Dome. She wanted her to come with us to Oklahoma City. We gave her to the Oklahoma authorities so she could get back to her parents. We hear she's back with them now.

As for us, we came to this area on our own, trying to find some way to get a house or something. First we stayed at a hotel. And they were kind of snotty with us. They cut all our phone lines off. We couldn't even make local calls. And then a friend of ours in California—she had the Internet. And she said she'd help us.

SIERRA: That's how they ended up finding HurricaneHousing. org and then me. My family and I live here in Stone Mountain, Georgia. To me, it was natural to take in Dennis and Michelle. I come from a really big family. When you have a family crisis and someone loses their apartment and they've got five kids you learn how to live with those situations. I'm the oldest of nine kids. So we're used to big numbers.

When we saw on TV what was happening with the hurricane, we just knew it was going to be devastating. I actually thought more people would die than did. It's easy to look at something like that and feel helpless. But I refuse to become helpless. Each one of us can do something even if it's very, very small. If everybody did one small thing, we wouldn't have such a big problem. Housing Dennis and Michelle is just my contribution to society. I owe that to myself and I owe it to the community I live in. This is the United States. And I'm a Native American. I come from Native American background, which is very communal.

My dad's Oneida. I grew up on the river basin in northwestern Montana. My grandparents were loggers. And they had to fight for the rights that make this country what it is. Most Native American people didn't even get citizenship until 1924. My grandmother was born not being able to be a citizen even though this was her homeland. So because of what my family's been through, being active as a citizen means something to me and I felt personally motivated to do something. I found HurricaneHousing. org on the Internet just by surfing. It took probably a week, a week and a half, to get a response.

I had no problem bringing strangers into the house. Whenever you have dinner together, you quit being strangers. Food is a universal thing. And speaking of which, little Alexia's not watching her noodles. (Laughter)

By the way, if you want to stay, it's spaghetti. There's plenty of it.

MICHELLE: We came over right after speaking for the first time. It felt good. It was a big relief to be somewhere else instead of being in a shelter or in the Dome. We've been here almost three weeks. It's nice, lovely. Everybody's getting along.

SIERRA: One of the first things I asked them was to feel comfortable, be at home. And then we discussed that if

[left to right] Sierra Mohawk (host), Searcie Cassidine (host's niece), Dennis Scott (evacuee), Mason Hayes (host's grandson), Michelle Peterson (evacuee), Eran Cassidine (host's niece)

we ever have any issues, let's talk about them. Let's not get mad at each other and go pout in the corner. I hate that. We can adjust things to try to meet everybody's needs as best as possible. Nobody is going to be perfectly comfortable. Sometimes there's going to be a line for the bathroom. That's just the way it is.

I feel sorry for Dennis 'cause it's all women. My grandkids come over, my daughter comes over, so it's not a whole lot of men that come around. I'm staying here, Susie's staying here and I think Eran's still upstairs doing her hair. ...

ERAN CASSIDINE: I'm right here.

SIERRA: Oh, she's down here, too. That's Eran. And those are her nieces. They both live here too.

DENNIS: I'm not complainin'. I mean, seriously, we'd gone through a real struggle. I am so grateful to be here right now.

SIERRA: Some of those stories you told me about the Superdome were very scary.

MICHELLE: Oh yeah. Like when everyone was trying to get out on buses. After a while things got so bad at the Dome that everybody was just trying to get out. Outside, they had these buses. But the guards were trying to separate the men from the women and children. And it wasn't happening. Nobody wanted to be separated from their family. They never said why they had to separate everybody like that.

So it got to the point where the guards had to pull the guns out to make everybody calm down. It was terrifying. All the children were going crazy, screamin' and cryin'. I felt sorry for the children more than anything.

And the conditions were just terrible. You had to use the bathroom outside. Or you had to pull a blanket over yourself and go to the bathroom in the corner. We ended up sleeping outside for many days.

SIERRA: Well, you're here now. And things are goin' okay. It's not easy, but we're takin' care of what needs to be done. Since these two have arrived, we've just been tryin' nonstop to deal with all the red tape of getting them some monetary support.

At least FEMA finally came through. They had these guys' checks floating around in Baton Rouge, sitting at the post office for quite a while. But those finally came through. We're still waiting for FEMA to help these two get signed up for public housing. The wait could be six months or longer.

MICHELLE: It's very frustrating that they can't tell us how long it will take.

DENNIS: It just takes so long to process. And they're so busy now. ...

SIERRA: Well, my commitment to you guys is open-ended. I'm here for you as long as it takes to get what you need. But I think we'll be able to find you a house and some furniture. I mean, I have a washer and dryer and a bed, a few other little odds and ends, sheets and towels and pans and stuff. It's just a matter of digging.

MICHELLE: And we're looking for work.

SIERRA: But it's not easy. There's a lot of red tape involved with all this stuff—stuff that would normally be simple. Down at the Red Cross, for instance, there was a lady who was trying to register her kids for school. And they're telling her she's got to have her child's shot records, she's got to have a withdrawal form from her child's old school.

And nobody in her situation has those things. But the people at the registration desk don't get that. To me, that's really frustrating.

We're dealing with people who are under so much stress. We can't have them just get frustrated and give up. People will get angry. People will just withdraw. So we've got to just keep trying as hard as we can to be understanding and flexible and really help these people.

MICHELLE: Well, we've been through a very, very hard time. But with people like Sierra out there, it gives us hope.

Can I read you something I wrote?

I'm a victim of Katrina. And this is my prayer:
Heavenly Father, please hear my cry.
Tell me why so many have died.
I come to you with my heart filled with pain.
Please shelter us from the rain.
I pray to you in this time of need.
Comfort your people, so their hearts won't bleed.
I'm on my knees for many a stress.
I was always told that my Father knows best.

Ease the hurt from all who grieve.
Let them know they must believe.
Rebuild the city with love once again.
I come to you in God's holy name. ⇨

Hurricane Katrina survivors temporarily sheltered in the Houston Astrodome.

"UNDER WHAT OTHER CIRCUMSTANCES would we ever be in the position to share the details of our lives? Under what other circumstances would we be able to kick back and realize that there are an awful lot of similarities between us?"

JERMAINE PAGE: I've lived in New Orleans all my life. I'm thirty-one. My mother is in Houston. My dad's in Chicago. My dad always lived in Chicago. My mother left before the storm. She was smart. She went to Baton Rouge first.

I was living in New Orleans, in the Uptown area, in some housing developments. I had done longshoreman work. I was working for Coastal Cargo Company, so we was off for a couple days prior. Me and my girlfriend and her kids were at home when the storm came, and we stayed and waited out the storm at the house. We caught a lot of winds, you know, big winds. I was on the third floor. The water came to the second floor, and I mean, these was some tall buildings. When we woke up that second morning and noticed it was steady rising, we decided we got to get out of there.

They was advertising that all evacuees can either go to the Superdome or the Convention Center and they will pick you up and take you to wherever. There were some families trapped on the first, second and third floors, and we managed to get them. We used air mattresses. We just floated those blow-up mattresses in the water between the first and second floor, bringing people out of the building on the mattresses. We took the older folks first.

We had some problems. There was a hole in one mattress, so we had to hold the hole shut the whole time. We'd put folks on a mattress, and three or four of the guys would float them down the road to the shallow part where you could actually walk. Back and forth like that. I'm 5' 8"

and sometimes the water was up to my neck. And I can't swim, but I was trying to help, bouncing up and down in the water, hopping in the water to try and stay afloat.

ELIZABETH CORNELL: You have to understand, Jermaine has a mortal fear of water, and here he is in chest-high toxic water with a child on his back. Wading through that water for miles. I made the mistake when he was first here of asking him, did he want to go swimming? And he said, "I don't want to be around water."

JERMAINE: And it was miles before we could actually get to dry ground. We had to walk pretty much half that day because, you know, we had elderly women that could barely walk.

It was twenty of us. We helped mostly women and children. We let half of them walk onto the Interstate. That's where we figured we would decide where to go next, because the Convention Center was a pretty far distance.

But we finally made it to the Convention Center. We were there for five days. It was like a jungle. It was just 20,000 black folks or more, just piled, you know, outside, inside the Convention Center, fending for themselves. It was just crime; it was just fighting. There was people that...that didn't make it, and we saw, like, sheets over...we thought it was just regular people resting but...once we got to talking to people, they said that's, you know, dead people.

They had a sheet over...well, they said that it was a baby.

At the Convention Center, every day they kept making us line up to get ready to board the bus. But, you know, those buses never did come. Finally, a National Guard helicopter arrived. We flew out and came to Kenner Airport in New Orleans, then took a Navy plane to Austin, Texas.

ELIZABETH: At the Austin Convention Center, there was between four and five thousand people.

JERMAINE: Which was a whole lot better than the Convention Center in New Orleans. There you had to fend for

[left to right] Jermaine Page (evacuee) and Elizabeth Cornell (host)

yourself. It was probably just due to people being uncomfortable and because it was so tight. It's so easy for people to get into conflicts under those conditions. You had to find toilets—nothing was provided for you. You had to go searching with your flashlight. When we was at the New Orleans Convention Center we had our own little section, and we actually had to have pipes and bats—trying to protect yourself and your people. Chaotic it was, you know.

After living in the Convention Center, once I got here, man, it was just a big relief. Coming to Austin, it was just so much love and support—more than we expected. It was just beautiful. Even in the Austin Convention Center. Anything we needed, they made sure we had it. It was overwhelming. They had the volunteers, they was working on getting housing for people.

I was with my girlfriend and her two boys. We parted, yeah, because we was going through things before the storm and during the storm. We were gonna split up before the storm anyway. But I wanted to make sure she was safe. I was making sure all of them got straight 'cause I knew I was going to be by myself. When she met up with her family at the Austin Center, I figured it was best she stay with them. So everybody got somewhere to go and I was the last one.

ELIZABETH: I'm an industry editor at Hoover's online. And my understanding was that there were all these people who had volunteered their beds in Austin through the HurricaneHousing website and there were all these people at the Convention Center, but there wasn't really any mechanism to hook these people up. So individual volunteers went down to the Convention Center, where they had so many computers set up. Sometimes they worked in pairs, as was the case with two women named Shelly and Sharon. Shelly was helping Jermaine and some other people get rooms. Sharon was trying to help people get registered with FEMA. The FEMA website was down unfortunately for days, so they just kept on trying over and over again.

As you can see, I've been pretty incapacitated due to my leg. But I've gotten so much help from people in the last couple of years that I just wanted to do whatever

it was that I could do beyond giving money. So I put my name on the housing donor list. Shelly called me on Tuesday and asked if she could bring Jermaine over that night. I said, "Yeah, sure." And she said, "Well, I'll call you back in a few minutes and let you know what the details are going to be." Shelly told me later that she hung up the phone and turned to Sharon and said, "This woman sounds pretty nice, she's up on Franklin Boulevard," which is only two blocks long. Sharon said, "I know somebody on Franklin Boulevard," and Shelly said, "This one is on crutches," and Sharon said, "That's Elizabeth Cornell." So we all figured it was meant to be. They called me back five minutes later.

I called a couple of family members and friends and they all said, "You're going to have a single man living in your house?" I could have specified a single woman or a family but I didn't care. I just said however many people could fit into one room. But my friends told me later that they were worried about me, and that none of them would have done it. But since then, my approval rating has gone up. (Laughs) Now they wouldn't be worried.

Jermaine and I clicked immediately, as soon as he got here. He walked in the door with a cheeseburger, and I said, "Sucker, now you got to take me to the grocery store because that's the hardest thing." The grocery store! (Laughs) I have a hard time with the supermarket cart.

JERMAINE: I had no problem with that, no problem. I enjoy doing that because she's done so much for me. I mean, she's helped me get a job. I'm working with the Goodwill. I thought it would be nice to be in that field, you know, helping out and dealing with donations and all that. I'm mostly doing stock work. And I started a morning thing with a friend of hers, helping him out. He does plumbing.

I'm really blessed to be here in this situation and Elizabeth has just been wonderful. I can't say enough about it. I'm able to focus. I'm able to at least try to get my mind set back on track, you know, from just being taken away like that. She's been a real big help.

ELIZABETH: He has met all my friends and everything.

JERMAINE: Yeah, she was taking me out and showing me good restaurants and all her friends. Very cool, you know what I'm saying? But like, after a week strong of just going out, I told her, I want to focus on working and getting stuff together. She wanted me to relax and, you know, take a couple days before I actually got off into what I got to do. But I didn't want to just lay up.

ELIZABETH: The first weekend that he was here, I was like, "You've made me the most popular person in Austin," because all these people had called and asked if we wanted to come over for dinner.

I learned a lot about New Orleans from Jermaine. I had no idea that New Orleans was as corrupt as it was. And I've also learned about the way that the entire system is kind of neatly interlocked to work against one man.

One thing that Jermaine told me the first night he was here, and I found this so weird, but he told me that when he got to the New Orleans Convention Center, there were all these people standing outside, of all races. And then when they got inside, the authorities separated everybody by race.

JERMAINE: Yeah, like, put the Vietnamese over here and the blacks over here.

ELIZABETH: He was saying, "Why didn't they just separate everybody by neighborhoods?" Because then at least you'd be able to see the people you knew and were familiar with.

JERMAINE: It'd be a community thing.

ELIZABETH: We've learned so much from each other in the short time that we've known each other. Three weeks. We obviously come from completely different backgrounds, but there are a lot of similarities in the ways that we grew up. I mean, on a higher level. And you know, we talk about politics, about how he could make a change in his community.

JERMAINE: And we talk about just being in New Orleans, the politics in the state, and how living there can be all kinds of crazy. I was trying to go somewhere and restart my life anyway. I actually envisioned in my mind to be in a specific place like this. And everything that's in the room is kind of how I wanted to start my life over. The computer, the bed. Just my own little room, clean and comfortable. But in order for me to start anew, I needed to leave everything. And start very small.

ELIZABETH: It's odd because I've lived alone now for a number of years and usually, when somebody is visiting me, I get a little uncomfortable after a few days, just because I need my space. You know, the three-day rule: "Visitors are like fish, they start stinking after three days." *(Laughs)* But this hasn't been that way at all. I think we're friends for life.

JERMAINE: Same here. Living here has been great. I mean, really, that month or two before it happened, I had been trying to get myself together, trying to just get somewhere.

Oh, man—it's wild in New Orleans, as far as trying to better yourself. There is nothing provided. And the corruption in the state goes all the way down to the New Orleans police. That's the reason why it took us five days to get here—because of the police corruption. I mean, they was talking about citizens looting, but in my opinion the police officers was looting more. Police officers was going into car dealerships and taking cars because their cars was running out of gas. So other guys was getting cars and trying to get out of there too, because no one was coming for us. Nobody was coming to help us.

Some guys I was with had a limo. And you know, we was starving, dying from thirst and lack of food and stuff. So we got into this store called Brown Velvet where they have water, orange juice, stuff like that. We load a whole limousine full of juices stacked the front to the back. So we going from spot to spot giving out juices and water. We made two trips like that. Handing out juices and water to the people outside the Convention Center. That made me feel good. That stuff was gonna go bad anyway and those people needed water and juice to survive.

We was gonna make a third trip when five officers come from behind the bushes with a gun. "Get out, get out," you know. I know they saw we was doing a good thing. It's not like we were joyriding or whatever. We was really helping. I mean, them people was clapping for us. The helicopter was flying the whole while, so we assumed the helicopter told them what we was doing was good. But they took the car and they rode off and no telling what they was doing.

Oh, and on Canal Street, see, they had guards. They had, like, police officers with guns on the street, and we thought they was just, you know, protecting. But as we was walking through the side street, we see police officers coming out with stuff, you know? And putting it in this van, you know what I'm saying? Not juice or water, but clothes, tennis shoes...Foot Locker, they were going in Foot Locker. Oh, man, it was crazy. They was actin' like criminals. And we were all suffering.

Before the storm there was a lot of police corruption. Selling drugs and stuff like that. I don't know if you know about the New Orleans police officers that are on death row right now. For murder—yeah, murdering, selling drugs, watching a drug warehouse and stuff like that, involved in drugs and hands-on with the criminals. It's just about as corrupt as it can get.

ELIZABETH: One thing that's kind of interesting, I think, between us, is that we are both in this situation where something external has hit the pause button in our lives. For me, for instance, I would love to change my job. There's so many changes in my life that I want to make, but I can't right now because I have to deal with this thing on my leg.

I'm wearing an external fixate around my leg. I have been lengthening my leg by a total of six inches over the last two years and I have this big honkin' machine on it right now. It looks like an Erector Set. And it's a good thing, but it's just going a lot more slowly than anybody expected it to. And I can't plan anything even for a year from now. I can't take commissioned freelance jobs writing, because I can't guarantee that six weeks from now I'm not going to be in the hospital when I have to turn in an assignment. Everything is on hold right now.

I used to have post-traumatic stress disorder, so I'm familiar with the signs. And in the beginning, I think Jermaine suffered from that. It was all part of him processing what he'd been through. At first he was very sensitive about racial issues. One night he asked me, "When was the first situation when you were the only white person in the room?" And I told him. Then I asked him, "When was the first time you were the only black person in the room?" And then I went, "Oh...I see...it's here."

This is a very white area. So I tried desperately to find other evacuee hosts so he could talk to someone from New Orleans, but I couldn't find anyone.

He was hypersensitive of his racial treatment. And there were incidents. Once he looked at an apartment, and I had told him it wasn't a good neighborhood for him, because you needed a car to live there and it was expensive. But the woman that was showing us around said to Jermaine, "All the apartments have cable, so you can watch your BET channel. And here's the basketball courts, I know how you people like to play basketball."

So I saw him go through that, and he saw me go through what I go through because of my leg. Because people feel like they have to say something to me. Once I was in a store and a woman said to me, "Why would you wear that in public?" And I said, "Well, I can't take it off. There are pins in it that go through my leg." But Jermaine was very protective of me in those situations. He got his back up about it a few times.

As a result of both our situations, we spurred each other on to overcome things. Jermaine has a daughter. She's fourteen, and in one of those weird twists of fate, she has *exactly* the same trouble with her leg that I have. From birth, her muscles were too short. She's had twenty surgeries, and I've had eighty-two. I really want Jermaine to reconnect with her. I want to tell her what I've been through. I want a chance to tell my "fourteen-year-old self" what I wish someone had told me.

I think we both share the kind of frustrations in having something beyond our control take over our lives. So it's been interesting talking about that stuff, too. I mean, it's obviously a totally different situation. But it's still...

JERMAINE: Yeah, that's how it was in New Orleans—so much I wanted to do and no easy way of doing it. The situation like this here, this is what I needed to get started. This is totally what I wanted. And it's because of Elizabeth, because of everything she has provided for me. She has a friend that's going to help me get back in school. All her friends, they're being there for me on account of her. Everything I needed in New Orleans, I'm getting here.

Before, in New Orleans, it was just an ongoing scandal, as far as the school system in the Ninth Ward and just, you know, money provided or opportunity basically.

ELIZABETH: Jermaine has a theory, that the one good thing that will come out of all this is that all those kids that were going to school in the Ninth Ward, that are now relocated in better places, will now have a chance at a good education. He thinks that will have an impact on this country.

I feel that as soon as Jermaine gets a permanent job that he can count on—because I don't think FEMA is going to come through with that much housing money— he'll be fine. He got a notice last week that said that they were going to investigate the housing that he was living in before and give him that much money for a life in Austin, which was what, a couple hundreds dollars a month for housing? The cost of living here is more expensive than New Orleans. I want Jermaine to feel comfortable staying here, but I want him to get a permanent job so he can save up some money.

JERMAINE: Austin kind of got a little similarity with New Orleans, with the music thing. I play the drums and she's got friends that play music. The city of New Orleans is known for the music, you know.

I started off in church years ago, but it led me to playing in school and once I got out of school I played a set with a jazz band. You see, my whole family got a lot of musicians—not famous, but local musicians. So I played with them at times, mostly like jazz, R&B. But I played a couple of tunes with the rock and roll thing, which I want to venture off into because it's so fast and, you know, you got to be on point, you know what I'm saying? That's what I want to focus on, learning how to play rock and roll.

All that is here for me. And don't they got a studio or something around the corner?

ELIZABETH: Yeah, there's a musicians' cooperative right around the corner. They took in a bunch of people. One of the Neville Brothers lives in there.

JERMAINE: Everything is right here. I want to stay busy, stay working, save money. I got to go back to my hometown, at least to visit. But I want a better life.

ELIZABETH: Jermaine and I are both single people around the same age. At first glance, one might think this is where the similarities between us end. He is a black male from the lower Ninth Ward in New Orleans. I am a white female, college-educated, who grew up in the upper middle-class. But Jermaine and I both realized on the second or third day we spent together that our meeting is a great big blessing in disguise. Under what other circumstances would we ever be in the position to share the details of our lives? Under what other circumstances would we be able to kick back and realize that there are an awful lot of similarities between us?

Though our adolescences were completely different, we still share life events that helped to shape us. Both of us are in the position of having an external force governing the immediate outcomes of our lives. The two of us are planning to chronicle our times together, so that we can keep track of the changes taking place for both of us. We both think this is a somewhat unusual story—but of course, there are no "usual" stories associated with Katrina, are there? ⇨

"WE HAD MOST OF OUR RELATIVES in New Orleans. I was born and raised there. I owned my own home. It makes a difference, when you own your own home."

JOSEPH DARBON: We're from New Orleans East. That's east of the downtown city. We evacuated the morning before the storm. It took us approximately twelve hours to go from New Orleans to Baton Rouge, which is eighty-five miles. An hour-and-a-half, on a normal day. We had a car, a Plymouth Voyager. But we couldn't find any hotel that had room. My aunt lives in Baton Rouge, so we stopped there. Later, we were joined by other relatives, so it was about fifteen of us in that house.

BARBARA DARBON: Four people already lived there, and they were already strained. The father had suffered a stroke and their son was paraplegic, so they were already on a pretty rigorous schedule. We tried to fit in as much as possible, tried to help out. We were kind of getting in the way though. We were there two days short of two weeks.

SONJA BARBER: I'm their daughter. From day one, I wanted them to come to Dallas, but we needed to find somewhere for them to live. I have a house in Garland, a suburb of Dallas, but it's really too small for all of us to live there.

My parents gave me a list of five or six different criteria I had to meet before they'd agree to move to Dallas. They needed a place with appliances for the kitchen. It had to be on the first floor. They needed a place where they didn't have to pay a down payment or sign a long lease. I looked in the *Dallas Morning News* and called a couple of places that were renting. They all wanted a bunch of things that didn't fit into the criteria. So then I went to HurricaneHousing.org. I work at EDS, Electronic Data

Systems in Plano, Texas and my manager actually sent the link out to everybody, in case anybody knew anybody who was affected.

I started scrolling down all the different entries until I came across Donna's entry. She'd said that she could house maybe two people for about a month or a little bit longer. She had different preferences. One was for a person with a little child. I understood that, because I'm a single mom, so I called her up, and right off the bat, we hit it off. I told her about my parents, and she thought that maybe they could be a good fit. Then I went through all the questions. "Do you have appliances? Yes. "Is it on the first floor?" Yes. Everything I asked her was a yes. Then Donna said she was willing to pay for the first month's rent for them...

DONNA ARCENEAUX: It had already been paid.

SONJA: See? She's so modest. She had already paid the September rent.

DONNA: Yeah, and into October some. Seven hundred forty-nine dollars a month. It's a nice middle-income-type working class neighborhood. It's officially a suburb of Dallas, but you'd never know it. The complex is at a busy intersection with a lot of access to public transportation. There's a grocery store, a Dollar store, restaurants, a post office not far away. I thought any family from New Orleans would appreciate having a grocery store within walking distance. I grew up in Houston, but my entire family is from south Louisiana for generations. So I feel connected to the area and to the people, culturally and spiritually.

I work for Corpus as an IT consultant and I'd just bought a new home. We'd lived in this apartment for two years, my daughter and I, but I still had a couple of months left on the lease, all paid out. I just felt like it would be a shame for this apartment to be vacant, with such a great need for housing for the people who were displaced. But it's not only that. I'm a single mom and we've gone through some rough times, and I've been lucky

[back row, left to right] Phillip Rayfield Brown V (son of evacuees), Sonja Barber (daughter of evacuees), Donna Arceneaux (host), Joseph Darbon (evacuee), Barbara Darbon (evacuee); [front row, left to right] Christopher Barber (Sonja's son), Anais Arceneaux-Donald (host's daughter)

enough to have people come into my life and help me. So instead of leaving, I just said, "I'm not vacating."

I found HurricaneHousing.org in some article I read on the Internet and went to the website and checked it out. It was about a week before Sonja emailed me. I hadn't had any other responses; I had criteria attached to my listing. I wanted a single mom or a young family with little kids, because I couldn't imagine being in a shelter somewhere with little kids. You need privacy. Or else I wanted an elderly couple, an older couple that needed to be in their own place. Vulnerable people who don't need to be in the general population of a shelter, where it's a kind of survival-of-the-fittest environment.

SONJA: I remember telling her that they're an elderly couple, but their four-year-old grandson will visit, so that counts as two of the kids! *(Laughter)*

DONNA: After talking with Sonja, I abandoned my hesitation. I just felt a real good bond with her and we seemed to understand each other, and everything was fine after that. I moved out of here on Labor Day weekend and then y'all moved in the weekend after that.

SONJA: And she wouldn't take any money for it. I'm thinking, okay, not only did they get everything they wanted, they don't have to pay the down payment and they don't have to sign a long contract either!

Mom and Dad were reluctant to come to Dallas. They were thinking they would go home, clean up the damage somehow. But while they're thinking that, I'm looking at the news. They had no electricity, so they didn't really know what was going on. But I had seen the pictures and I'd been to the websites where people were saying that there was up to fifteen feet of water where my parents lived. I knew they didn't have anywhere to go back to, but I didn't want to tell 'em that.

BARBARA: She's saying come to Dallas, and Joseph was saying we got to go back and tend to our property. Then the news of the levee came. We lived right by the levee. Our home is destroyed and we can only afford about $500 a month for rent. What do we do?

SONJA: I'm thinking, *Dallas at $500 a month!?* And then Donna just appeared like an angel!

JOSEPH: We were debating at first. Should we go? You have to take one day at a time.

BARBARA: To me, everything's in God's hands. I trusted Sonja's judgment, and then when we got here, it was beyond my expectations.

I'd been hearing stories, from other evacuees, about the outpourings of kindness from people, but you never really think it's gonna happen to you. And when it does happen to you, it's like, "What did I do to deserve this?" I feel the Lord leaned on a heart, to have her there at the right time for us.

DONNA: I think there's a reason we all came to each other's lives.

BARBARA: We really clicked.

DONNA: We really did. Everything just worked out beautifully. And you know, my daughter has a lot of questions, and Barbara has given her a good history lesson about the hurricane in New Orleans and the history of the state and how politics are there, because my daughter asked her, "Well, where was the President?" *(Laughter)*

BARBARA: And I said, "That's what I wanted to know. That's what we were all wondering." *(Laughter)*

JOSEPH: I tell people I've been around the world five times and spoke to everybody twice. You know? I was a tech sergeant in the Air Force. I've seen poverty, like in Vietnam, places like that, but I've never seen anything quite like this evacuation from Hurricane Katrina. In a war zone, you find kids who don't know where their parents are. Parents don't know where their children are. You find people who are wounded, sick, people who are dying or being killed, and all of these things. But when you see something like this happening here at home in America...well, it's unbelievable.

You go from being a person who can give to others to the other end, where *you* have to receive. The receiving part... is very difficult. We've never been there before. I've been on my own since I was seventeen years old. I've been places like Germany, England, Spain. I went to France and stayed in a hotel for about three or four weeks, and had to come take my kids and my wife to the base to eat breakfast, dinner and supper, and I never needed nobody to give me a hand for any of this stuff. It's kind of difficult. Being on the receiving end.

We had most of our relatives in New Orleans. I was born and raised there. I owned my own home. It makes a difference when you own your own home. Anywhere you go, wherever, there's no place like home. So it's just been difficult.

DONNA: Look, these people have worked hard. They'd retired, they had their pensions, insurance, a comfortable brick home, a nice van. They'd raised all these children— and they'd always been there when their kids needed help. It's just been really tough for them to accept charity.

BARBARA: When Donna comes by, she always wants to do more, and I keep going, "But you got me this far. I can take it from here."

SONJA: Donna continues to do things for them. Almost daily.

BARBARA: She's bringing us food and clothes from her church.

DONNA: I was really proud of my church, Holy Cross. We turned one of the classrooms into a donation center. We collected really nice quality, beautiful clothes, blankets, food. One Sunday they collected frozen chickens! All kinds of really good stuff.

BARBARA: It's like, "Well Donna, just calm down!" (*Laughs*)

JOSEPH: She gave me a ladder, you know? (*Laughs*) She gave me a ladder!

SONJA: I think it's awesome. What they're saying about how they've never had to be on the receiving end is true. I told them about the apartment and Donna just to get them up here. I didn't tell them that my church, the Free Will Church in Garland, was completely furnishing their apartment, because I knew that would kind of scare them off. Then the first day we got here, as we stood outside the door, I said, "I have not been completely honest with y'all. There's something I didn't tell you." My Dad said, "So you're gonna live here too?" I said, "No, I'm not gonna live here. But when you walk through the door, everything you see in that apartment, my church came last night and put it there. I just want y'all to know that it's all yours."

When they came through the door, and they just couldn't believe it.

JOSEPH: The church brought that television right there. Brand-new in a box. Twenty-seven-inch.

BARBARA: We got everything. Dishes, pots and pans, glasses. I mean, I was expecting nothing and it's almost like I moved into a resort or something! Don't pinch me, because I don't want to wake up!

JOSEPH: I told one of 'em last night, when he brought this table here and two little coffee tables, "I don't know how long we're gonna be here or what I'm gonna do with all this stuff." He said, "Look, just call the church and tell 'em you need the moving ministry. They'll send somebody out to pack everything up and move it on the truck, and move it for you." Now what do you think about that?!

BARBARA: I don't mean to sound too spiritual, honey, but it's like the Lord just used all these instruments. It just overflows me. I personally have three lessons I can testify to. First is my family. We have everybody accounted for. Secondly, we didn't have to go to that Superdome shelter. Third was to have a place like this to come to. I'm still trying to adjust.

SONJA: My whole life, my mom took care of me, and for the last twenty years, my dad's taken care of me. They got married when I was in college—my biological father was in the Air Force too—but my mom was a single mom for over ten years and I never wanted for one single thing. I didn't know it at the time, but apparently we were poor. My mom was a bank teller and I thought bank tellers made a lot of money. Until I became an auditor and found out, no, they really don't.

My mom bought us a house. We always had a car. When I said we were poor, I just mean we couldn't go to the mall shopping, but we had everything spiritual that we needed and my mom always sacrificed. I didn't know other people's moms didn't wear a coat for ten years and then when I would outgrow my coat, my mom would wear it. I just thought that was normal. I always got new clothes and I just thought your mom wasn't supposed to. When I got to college, I found out that a lot of moms don't even care about their kids, much less sacrifice for them.

So I had to do this for them. And Donna does so much for them. Things I wouldn't even think of!

DONNA: I'm outside of the situation. It's easier for me to see things. When I met her parents, that Sunday evening, they were all settled in and happy to be there and they gave me a big hug. They were just open, warm people, very grateful and well-spoken. I felt totally at home. Every time we go over, they offer us something to eat, some good fish or something cooked Louisiana-style.

SONJA: I told Donna, "Well, they'll just adopt you as a daughter," because that works. I never had a sister, so I'll just go with that. I've been good and spoiled for the first forty years. I can share the fame now! *(Laughs)*

JOSEPH: The biggest problem now, we got cell phones, but half the time, we can't get through or somebody calls us and they can't get to us. It's frustrating. I'd put a telephone in here, but we don't even know how long we're gonna be here. One day at a time. When people ask me where I'm from, I say I'm from New Orleans. I come from the City of Love and the State of Confusion.

BARBARA: We can't get FEMA on the phone. We can't get them on the phone.

DONNA: That's kind of why I keep bringing stuff and doing stuff. I didn't want them to feel like they're out there dealing with big bad FEMA alone. I thought this would be a good, safe place for someone vulnerable. It's got an alarm. It's gated. Everything is very nice for people who stay here to be safe. And we'll be friends for the rest of our lives.

SONJA: And our kids will grow up and be friends. They'll grow up together. ⇨

"IT TOOK EVERYTHING OUT OF ME TO be turned away after not being able to provide any assistance, when I knew how much we could have helped."

KATHLEEN MCCULLOUGH: I work for the Federal Aviation Administration. Right after the hurricane passed, we got a call-out to drive to Baton Rouge: "Baton Rouge Airport needs generators and diesel fuel. Drive and do not stop." So that's what we did. We arrived very early Thursday morning, so the storm had already come and gone. I repair instrument landing systems, navigational aides, communications and things like that. Initially, Baton Rouge Airport did not have full commercial power, but when we arrived, power had been restored and the generators were no longer needed there. One of the coordinating FAA technicians told us to just park the generators and go get some sleep.

On the drive down to Baton Rouge, I had been listening to the morning radio shows. And I heard more and more people calling in asking for diesel fuel to run generators, to run hospitals and nursing homes in New Orleans. And not just New Orleans proper, but some of the hardest hit areas, like Slidell. Most of the people that called in asking for fuel were told to call the Red Cross. So the next morning, I was watching the TV in the motel room and I could see, again, that the need for fuel in New Orleans was great. And we had hundreds of gallons of diesel that I knew someone could use.

At a minimum, I knew that there were people that needed that fuel or needed the generators. Trying to find out who was in charge, trying to find *someone* who could make decisions, was a complete and absolute debacle. Communication in and out of New Orleans was scattered at best. There was no coordinated inter-agency communication, which was *supposed* to come from FEMA.

At a local, state and federal level, everyone was looking for guidance from FEMA. For instance, was it okay for me to turn over FAA fuel to the Coast Guard? Or to anyone going into New Orleans? In theory, FEMA should be making that decision. But we couldn't find anyone from FEMA at Baton Rouge Airport. There was no protocol beyond my own agency, at my level, to contact or suggest or move any ideas except through FEMA. When FEMA went under the Department of Homeland Security structure, they became the go-to people for this kind of disaster guidance. But these guys were nowhere around. So the FAA said, "Leave that decision to FEMA." Well, nobody could find FEMA.

You know, the entire trip down there, I didn't pass one military convoy. I passed a couple of buses and I didn't see anybody coming back. I just kept hearing on the radio: "Help is on the way! Help is on the way!" And I'm just sitting there thinking, *There's no help coming. I just drove I-10. There's nothing on it.* This is already days into the hurricane, or the aftermath.

At Baton Rouge Airport, there were Chinook helicopters and Blackhawk helicopters and a row of Coast Guard life-rescue boats parked right there. They were on trailers, just in a row, parked. There was nobody to talk to; there was no action.

I was pretty frustrated. And disgusted. It took everything out of me to be turned away after not being able to provide any assistance, when I knew how much we could have helped. What if that fuel could have kept a hospital running? What if?

See, the FAA is incredibly efficient. One of the problems of a national tragedy like this—or any hurricane or a tornado—is that they generally damage the navigational

[left to right] Roxann Stewart (evacuee), Kathleen McCullough (host), Jennifer Sexton (host)

aides at airports. The navigational aides radiate the signal that aircraft use to centerline on a runway. No one can land a plane without operational navigational aides. Now, the FAA's response time for getting those navigational aides back up and operating is phenomenal. It's lightning speed. They can assemble crews from all over the United States if need be. If Corpus Christi gets hit, then employees from the Southwest region and surrounding System Management Offices will go there immediately to provide technicians. We get airports up and running fast.

After Katrina, FAA personnel had Louis Armstrong Airport restored in record time. So it wasn't the FAA saying, "You can't land at this airport." That airport was operational; it was ready to go! And when President Bush landed there days later and said, "Help is on the way," they did one of the biggest airlifts ever out of that airport. *But they could have been doing it days before.* I don't get it. We did our job. Everything was ready. What took so long? The sky was full of helicopters. The airports were operational and had been ready for days to evacuate people. But noth-

ing was coming through, with the exception of a small Coast Guard crew that was operating to rescue people off rooftops and things like that.

We were capable of doing so much more. We could have worked in forty-eight-hour shifts—I know I would have. There could have been airliners shuttling people in and out.

You know, we can go and drop troops into Iraq in a day. I was in the Marine Corps; we can deploy in less than twenty-four hours, and we're on the other side of the world.

There's all this coverage on TV and the radio about what is needed. How are the people at the top missing the obvious? How are they so out of touch? Why were those people left at the Dome in harm's way, to starve and thirst?

FEMA was saying it's a National Guard issue. The National Guard was saying it's a FEMA issue. Ah, we were so close to bringing generators into New Orleans.

There were two checkpoint numbers and there were armed guardsmen that were guarding the entrance into

New Orleans. And you had to call those checkpoints before you proceeded into the city. The afternoon that I was there is the same day that the supposed shots got fired at a helicopter and the word finally came down: "Pull out." Word from who? That's a question for the Congressional Hearing Committee. People like my boss can't send people voluntarily into what had escalated into a dangerous situation. They can't do that. Whenever that incident with the shots happened, the word came down to pull out.

But what was really true? What was real and what was fiction? There was a report of riots in Baton Rouge. But then someone called in on the radio and said, "Stop spreading rumors. There is no riot." So it was hard to separate fact from fiction. Someone issued an order to leave, so that's it—state, local and federal employees are pulling out of the city.

And that was an absolute directive. We are pulling out of the city. And so I was just standing there saying, "I'm willing to stay and help, you just tell me where to go." And nobody had an answer.

And of course, I wasn't the only one. All kinds of people were showing up, trying to help. There were pilots calling in to the flight service stations to find out how to get a flight plan into New Orleans and they were told, "No." The minute that happened some of our controllers from Mississippi called FEMA to question this and they were told, "We'll get back to you."

Why would someone do that? When I was driving back, I called my mother and I was just...just sobbing. I said, "I don't know...is it because they're poor and because they're black that nobody at the top cares?"

You can't tell me nobody had the foresight to make those decisions for Katrina. You can't tell me there's a gray area here about whether this was a state or a federal issue. Look, if a nuclear warhead is launched and heading for the city of Los Angeles—do we all shrug our shoulders and say, "I'm sorry, but that's clearly a Los Angeles city problem?" When something like this impacts the *nation*, it ceases to be a state or a local issue. It becomes absolutely federal.

So when I came back from Baton Rouge, I was completely disenfranchised with how the situation was getting handled. And I was angry. Jen approached me, and she said, "What do you think about opening up our house to somebody who really needs it?" And I said, "Well, I was kinda thinking about it, but I was reluctant to ask."

I wanted to help someone very badly, but we had just taken an individual into our home a while back—a person who had lost her job. We were trying to help her get back on her feet. Anyway, it turned out to be a bad experience and I didn't want to say, "Let's just gamble again and see what happens." I didn't want to do that to Jen. But Jen said, "Well, let's see if we can put somebody up who has every capability to have a job and be employed." So we went online and I ended up on the MoveOn.org website and that directed me to HurricaneHousing.org. I just put something very basic up. It said: "There's one bedroom in our home, with a vehicle for use."

We got Roxann's email within a couple of hours. She explained that she was a displaced student and wanted to get on a campus here in Dallas. We just started emailing back and forth. It was quite a few days before we had our first phone conversation, but I got a really good sense that it was the right thing to do. So she came out and she's been a part of our house. I don't like to consider her an evacuee or any of the other terms. She's a very, very awesome roommate. And it's really turned out great.

She's been through a lot and this is a big change for her, of course. We try to take her out with us all the time, out with friends and to dinner.

ROXANN STEWART: Because most of the time I just sit and sulk. (*Laughter*)

No, it's true. Sometimes I'm just depressed. Sometimes. Not often. It's...having to move from home and be here without anybody that I can directly relate to. It's kinda hard, because at home there was always somebody that I could go see, go do stuff with. And out here...well, first of all, I don't know how to get nowhere. And then I don't have anybody to go with, because these two are a team! They come as package (*Laughter*)

I mean, you know, I'm a single. I'm a twenty-ounce; I come alone. So dealing with feeling alone on top of everything else that's on my plate...it's hard.

If I can go to school, I'm happy. I love school. I transferred from Southern University in New Orleans to Argosy here in Dallas. It's a problem, because college is expensive and I like to take a lot of classes to keep myself busy. Learning is fun for me and people call me a nerd, but whatever. It's fun for me, and if I can go to school, I'm happy. So being able to live here with Kat and Jennifer... well, I feel blessed. And just be here, you know, without anything expected of me.

My family home is ruined by the storm—water and mold. I miss it. But most of it is just missing being *at* home. I still call my mama every day, but it's not the same. My sister's birthday is coming up and I'm gonna end up missing her birthday, because I have class. But I'm gonna try to see if I can spend the week at home for my birthday because I don't know nobody. Just me, Jen and Kat can't have no party.

KAT: Hey, we can throw a party...

JENNIFER SEXTON: Make the cats wear little hats; it'll be all right. (*Laughter*)

Roxann helps us out all the time and that takes a little bit of the pressure off me. Because I go to nursing school Monday through Friday, forty hours a week, just like a job.

KAT: And I work forty hours a week and I'm taking fifteen hours right now of college to work on my electrical engineering degree. We love having her around.

JENNIFER: And she can actually cook!

KAT: Hey, I cook.

JENNIFER: I'm just teasing!

ROXANN: The first thing that I cooked was...

JENNIFER: The baked ziti, I think that was the first thing.

KAT: Oh yeah.

ROXANN: I don't like jambalaya, but I know how to make it. If they wanted it, then I would be able to make, but I don't like it.

JENNIFER: That fried chicken was good. That was the best damn fried chicken I've ever had.

ROXANN: If you wanna eat it, I can probably cook it.

JENNIFER: Roxann's a great cook. She says, "I'm all right." And I'm like, "Oh, no. You don't understand. We live on taquitos and pizza."

KAT: Look, I know what it's like to not be around your family. So it's hard for me, because I want Roxann to be happy. I know that it's hard for her not to be able to just call somebody up and say, hey, let's go out and you know, talk about New Orleans. So that part's difficult. You can have this great environment, but without your family and your friends? All the money in the world doesn't mean anything without that.

ROXANN: But you know, this is my support system now. And when I need somebody to talk to, I just fill Kat's ear up or fill Jen's ear up—and they listen. I don't have anybody but these two. I owe them a lot for this. There is no way I can repay them. Money won't even do it, because not only did they take me in and give me a place to stay. They are my friends. They took me in when I needed them, and I'll never forget it. ⇨

DEAN HUETTMANN: I'm a pharmacist. I lived in Arabi, New Orleans. That's in St. Bernard Parish. I stayed through the storm and had to get rescued off my roof. My wife and son and daughter had already evacuated. A boat from the fire department came around and got me off my roof and took me to St. Bernard's prison—cellblocks, the whole thing. Everybody was crowded in there. Bad, bad conditions. But it was the only dry spot in St. Bernard Parish. I finally got reunited with my family in Houston, Texas.

We had no computer access. We could log on for an hour a day at the library, but we spent most of that time trying to get hold of FEMA. A friend of my wife's from Washington state logged onto HurricaneHousing.org and found Dottie and Norman for us.

NORMAN KRUSTCHINSKY: We've had this spare cottage for rent for a while now. We kept wondering why it didn't rent. Now we know why. We needed to get it ready for Dean and his family.

DOTTIE KRUSTCHINSKY: God works in mysterious ways.

NORMAN: Oh, He surely does. ⇨

[back row, left to right] Aaron Huettmann (evacuee's son), Dean Huettman (evacuee);
[front row, left to right]: Norman Krustchinsky (host), Dotti Krustchinsky (host)

"I CLICKED ON LYNN'S POSTING AND I read it out loud to my six-year-old son Daylen. When Daylen heard it he was just like, "She has two dogs and a bird? Two dogs and a bird, momma! I hope you respond to that one!" And I said, "Yes I did."

PATRICE BRIANT: We lived in a section of New Orleans called Mid-City, in a two-bedroom home that we'd just moved into a few months ago. We moved there from a home that we'd actually owned and then ended up losing.

Crazy as it sounds, the house we owned was damaged from another storm that happened two years previously. We lost insurance on the house and it just fell into a state of disrepair to the point that we couldn't live in it anymore. Losing that place was very hard, but, looking back, I honestly thank God that we weren't living there when Katrina hit, because that old house has water up to the roof right now. Who knows if we would've gotten out?

Our most recent home was owned by a wonderful French gentleman who'd just renovated the whole thing top to bottom. It was the most beautiful house you'd ever want to see. And we had just settled in—my husband David and I and our three children. The kids had just started school. David was working as a paralegal for the City Attorney's office. And I was out on disability from my job as Human Resources Manager for the Château Sonesta Hotel. I was diagnosed with degenerative bone disease, so that had put me out of work for a while.

The fact that I'd worked for the Château Sonesta, a nice hotel on Canal Street in New Orleans, was gonna be a big help to us during the storm 'cause we'd have been able to stay there for free. That's where we sat out Hurricane Ivan. And the Sunday before Katrina hit, our intention was to stay there with my two sisters and my mother, who's got a lung condition. She actually has holes in her lungs for some reason. She doesn't smoke or anything like that. It's just some weird disease. And it's required her to be on oxygen for the past six years. So you can imagine how difficult it would be to move my mother out of the city.

But, for some reason, at the last minute, I just decided I was not gonna stay. I honestly don't know what it was but I just wanted to drive somewhere far away. So I packed up, put my kids in the car and just left. My mother would be safe at the hotel, or so I thought.

As it turned out, that was not the case. My sisters had made reservations at the hotel the day before. But when they arrived there with my mother, the hotel told them the reservations had been cancelled and that they'd have to go to the Superdome.

I knew if my mother went to the Superdome she would die. So when I got that call on my cell phone explaining the situation, I just had to turn back. It didn't matter how many hours I'd been driving. So I went back to that hotel and gave them a piece of my mind. Oh *yes* I did. (*Laughs*) And they ended up letting my mother and two of my sisters stay at the hotel.

Two of my other sisters though ended up going to the Superdome. And the situation there was just ugly. Sitting on that line to get into the Dome, they were literally spit on and threatened with guns because people wanted their place in line. 'Cause the deal was, once you were in the line, if you stepped out, you'd lose your spot. The National Guard would put you out. I mean, the National Guard was just overwhelmed. 'Cause the New Orleans police were nowhere to be found—some of them actually walked off the job. And there were about 100,000 people outside that

[back row, left to right] Lynn Viejobueno (host), Patrice Briant (evacuee), David Briant (evacuee); [front row, left to right] Michelle Briant (evacuee), Daylen Briant (evacuee), Mariah Briant (evacuee)

Convention Center, all tryin' to get *in*. To manage a group of people that large with no local police—it was chaos.

So you couldn't leave that line for anything, not even to eat or use the bathroom. And my sisters stood there for forty-eight hours. I mean, they were literally forced to soil themselves just to stay in that line. By the time I finally re-united with those two sisters here in Texas, they were just hysterical. I almost didn't even recognize them. You could just see it on their faces what they'd been through.

I mean, David and the kids and I got an idea of what they were going through as we left, because to get out of town we needed to drive past the Superdome. And as we passed by we just a saw thousands of people stranded outside. And Daylen, my youngest child—he's six—he just started crying. He was hysterical. He knew something very bad was going on. But we just kept driving. I think we drove for...maybe about twelve hours? That's how long it took us to get to Jackson, Mississippi.

DAVID BRIANT: Oh yep, a long time actually. What we were going to do was head west. But when I got to High-way 90, I had to turn around because the lines were so long. We had to go all the way back to New Orleans East. And that took a long time. You can probably imagine the traffic. It was bad.

But we finally crossed the Twin Spans and kept on going. If you've seen the pictures on TV, you'll know that those bridges we crossed over to get out of town over Lake Pontchartrain are collapsed now.

PATRICE: The weather started getting real bad as we were heading out. On our way to Jackson, we stopped at about nine hotels, none of which had any rooms. And eventually it got to be about one-thirty in the morning. The storm was picking up and Daylen started having an asthma at-tack. So we stopped at another hotel and David went in to ask if we could plug Daylen's asthma machine in, so I could give him some medication.

In the meantime, while David was doing that, a gentleman comes up and says "Do you guys need a room? Because we have two rooms and I can give them to you." He was there with another gentleman on a business trip and they just wanted to get back home to Memphis,

where they were from, before things got any worse. And he overheard our situation and was good enough to let us have his rooms. He paid for that night for us. So we stayed in the hotel for free. He was the first of many gracious people who came to our aid.

I never even got that nice man's name. Tried to call the hotel to ask so I could thank him, but they wouldn't give it to me. There was just too much going on.

Anyway, we stayed at the hotel that night and then the next. And just before the power went out at the hotel, my sister called and told me my mother—who was still at the hotel at this point—only had twelve hours of oxygen left on her tank. And once the oxygen runs out, she would die.

So I knew that I had to go back home again to save my mother's life.

DAVID: But with the power bein' out in Jackson, Mississippi, we didn't know about the levees breaking in New Orleans. There was no television for us to watch the news. No radio either. So we had no idea what was going on.

PATRICE: We had no idea that it would be impossible to get back into New Orleans. And I needed to save my mother. So we started heading back. We pulled off at every little pit stop from Jackson Mississippi to—how far did we get? Covington?

DAVID: Hammond.

PATRICE: Hammond. I was stopping at every little mom-and-pop gas station tryin' to call whoever might be able to help. I stopped and called the National Guard, the Red Cross, just trying to get through to someone who could help my mother.

I finally got through to the National Guard and they said they were gonna put my mother on a waiting list of some sort. Then I got through to the Red Cross and they put her name on another list. So things were startin' to look a little better. But they told me there were thousands of other people they were tryin' to rescue. So I was still very worried.

We kept on driving. And then at Covington, the po-lice made us turn around. I knew my sister's in-laws lived in Baton Rouge, but I didn't know where. All the same, we headed to Baton Rouge in hopes of finding them. So on our way, we made it to a Burger King out in the middle of nowhere. I had to plug my cell phone in because the battery was dead and I couldn't call anybody for help anymore. They let me plug the cell phone in and charge it and they gave us some free drinks. And then out of nowhere this man comes in and overhears us talking about everything that happened. And the next thing you know he just gives us a hundred dollars out of nowhere and told us if we needed any additional assistance to give him a call. He was our second angel.

When I finally got my cell phone up and working I was finally able to reach my sister's daughter, who lives in Atlanta. And she gave me directions to the in-laws' house. And when we arrived, we found around thirty members of my sister's husband's family staying there, including three pregnant women. So needless to say it was overcrowded. You had all these people running around—it was just chaos. But at least we were able to use a phone and try to find where my mother was and see how my sisters were doing.

When I finally reached my sisters, I found out that my mother had been airlifted to a hospital in Baton Rouge. She had deteriorated quite a bit, but she was alive. And I just thanked God for that.

We stayed at that house for a week, but there was no room inside for us to sleep. So we slept in the car—five people in a Ford Escort. And I have serious major back issues. After a week, I just got to the point where I could not tolerate sleeping in the car or on the floor anymore. So we had to leave the kids at the house and drive around from shelter to shelter tryin' to find somebody that had space available in Baton Rouge. Basically, it was impossible because most of the people who evacuated from New Orleans had no money and Baton Rouge was the closest place. So no shelters were open.

DAVID: There were lines for everything.

PATRICE: Every place we went there were people already standin' in line waiting for space. But at one of the shelters—Bethany Church—a worker there told me "go to this website." And it was HurricaneHousing.org.

Back at my sister's in-laws' house, I got on their computer late at night and went to the website and just clicked on Houston, because my husband's brother lives in Spring, Texas. I said to myself, *At least there will be family not too far away.* And the first house I clicked on happened to be Lynn's, believe it or not.

LYNN VIEJOBUENO: And it was probably like five minutes after I posted it.

PATRICE: I clicked on Lynn's posting and read it out loud to my six-year-old son old son Daylen. When Daylen heard it he was just like, "She has two dogs and a bird!? I hope you respond to that one!" And I said, "Yes, I did." But I also said to myself, *There are probably hundreds or thousands of people who've responded to that same ad. So we've just gotta cross our fingers and wait and pray and hope somebody calls.*

LYNN: And I did call!

I'd been watching the hurricane on the news. And I just felt like I needed to help in some way. My daughter and I had taken all our extra clothing to the Katy Christian Ministries. And then we went and bought some gift cards from Wal-Mart and took them over to a Red Cross shelter. In Wal-Mart, we saw all these people shopping for shoes and basic clothes. And then, seeing all the Louisiana plates out in the parking lot, we realized that all these people had just fled the hurricane. And they'd lost everything. And I was asking myself, "My God, what more can I do? I mean, I've already given clothes. And I don't have money to give." I'm a real estate agent, but around here that's not exactly a high-income profession.

But the thing is, I'm recently separated from my husband. I have a home in California and one in Colorado. And I just bought this one, here in Katy, Texas, last March. I'm waiting for my house in California to sell. And that's why I'm sort of camping out here with just the bare necessities. Anyways I started thinking, "I'm sitting in this *big house* alone." There's gotta be some way to make use of all this empty space. I have a large area upstairs—three bedrooms, two bathrooms. So I was in the perfect position to help out some people in need. I went to the computer and somehow, some way I got to HurricaneHousing.org.

I had never heard of MoveOn.org before. I don't know how I found it, to be quite honest with you, but I got it. And I posted my little ad.

On the screen, it said you might not hear from anybody for two weeks. So I thought, *okay, fine.* But in a matter of thirty minutes I got a call from one lady. She was up at the Reliant Center. Then I got calls from numerous other people, but some of 'em were, like, families of *twenty-two.* So after a few situations that didn't work out, I got Patrice's email. And it just made me burst into tears. Her family was *living in a car.* I was so happy to be able to call Patrice and take her family into my home.

PATRICE: The morning we got the call, I had just come back from standing in a line for the Red Cross. And I was so depressed because we didn't get anywhere. They cut the line off *three people* before us and told us to come back tomorrow. By the time I got back to my sister's in-laws, I was this close to starting to cry. Because everything just kept falling apart.

LYNN: When I called I actually talked to Mariah first.

PATRICE: Mariah came up to me, holding the phone and said, "Mommy, it's the lady with the bird and the dogs!" (*Laughter*)

When she told me Lynn had called—I don't know what I had in my hand, but I dropped everything. And the next day we were driving to Lynn's.

We're lucky the car even made it. A mechanic that we'd met offered to check it for us for free before we left. So many people helped us along the way. But we made it. Thank God. And now I'm so grateful.

I mean, it was just so important for me to get my kids to a place where...you know, this is Michelle's senior year in high school.

LYNN: And that was another thing that got to me. Not only was there a family of five living in a Ford Escort. But you know, Michelle is a senior. And I felt so bad for her. Your senior year is supposed to be special. And hers has just been shot. But the school district here is fabulous. Of course it can't replace her original school, but I think Michelle ended up at least with second best.

MARIAH BRIANT: I was so angry. Because I finally got into a school I liked and then I had to leave.

PATRICE: It was a school for the gifted. The schools that my children were in were both schools for gifted and talented children—two of the best schools in the city of New Orleans. Michelle sings opera and plays piano. She was supposed to have her senior recital next spring. And now that's not gonna happen. But at least we've found her another good place to go.

MICHELLE BRIANT: I was so sad at first, when I had to leave my school. But I haven't been down lately. At first I was worried about catching up but now I think I'll be okay. Eventually, later in the semester, I'm going to have to go back over things that they covered before I got here. I missed four weeks. But I'm catching up. And everybody I talk to has it pretty nice here. I made a lot of friends. I even found someone at my new school who was a senior at my old one. He got there about a week before me. It was really nice to see a familiar face.

LYNN: They have a nice group of kids here. And the schools have support groups. Because there are a lot of kids here now from New Orleans who were victims of Katrina.

MICHELLE: I'm actually supposed to attend one of those support groups tomorrow.

PATRICE: I'm sure you'll meet some more nice people there. I mean, practically everyone we've met since we've arrived in Texas has been nice to us. And we were so nervous before we got here. I mean, we were moving into a stranger's house. We just didn't know what to expect. The day we drove to Lynn's house for the first time, I was talking to David and the kids, saying, "She sounds really sweet over the phone. I'm sure she's a really nice person."

LYNN: They were also cutting jokes about me being some weird lady with stuffed pets. (*Laughter*)

PATRICE: The kids were joking, saying, "Well mom, she has two dogs and a bird. What if they're not really alive? What if they're stuffed? What if she's crazy?!" And all I was thinking was, *even if she is crazy, it'll be better than the five of us living in a Ford Escort.*

LYNN: Hey, it's five of you and one of me! (*Laughs*)

PATRICE: Aw, we were just nervous! But when we got here Lynn was just like, "Hey, welcome!" She just put us at ease. We were so relieved.

But then the *next* hurricane came. A few days later, Hurricane Rita came right here to Lynn's house.

We heard Rita was approaching. At first I thought, *Well, we're in Houston, far away from the coast. We'll be fine.* Then it went from Category Three to Category Four and I said to myself, *Okay, I'm gettin' a little nervous.* And then it went from Category Four to Category Five and it was the whole Katrina thing all over again. And I have to admit—I'll admit this to you—I sat here the day before the storm hit and I just freaked out. I honestly could barely take it at that point. I was just like, "Damn, not again. We just got here. And now we're going to lose *this* house. We have to go somewhere else. But we have nowhere else to go." And I finally cracked up. I just broke down crying. Lynn wasn't here. She was on the road.

LYNN: What happened with me was, my mother is seventy-nine years old and, like Patrice's mom, she's on oxygen. And my daughter was worried about Hurricane Rita knocking the power out and disabling mom's oxygen, like what happened with Patrice's mom. So I agreed to help my daughter and we put Mom's oxygen into a van and headed north. I left Patrice and her family at my house alone.

PATRICE: In the end, we didn't even get any rain. We got wind. But I was still so afraid that something worse was going to come. You can ask David—he was about to slap me. I was running around here that day screaming and yelling the whole time. He has experience blocking me out, so he probably didn't pay any mind. But nothing happened. I was relieved. I did a lot of praying. I wasn't really a religious person before Hurricane Katrina, but after all the praying I've done—for my home, my family, my mother—I feel like I am now.

LYNN: Well, Patrice, maybe it worked! Anyway, it's a good thing you didn't go because Rita turned out to not be so bad.

PATRICE: Well, Lynn, we would've taken you with us!

LYNN: We have a little boat in the garage. We could have rowed somewhere! (*Laughter*)

PATRICE: But seriously, I'm a strong believer now. I strongly believe it's a miracle that all these things happened and that all these people helped us. It was a miracle finding Lynn. It's a miracle that my mother is still alive, it's a miracle that I even know where all my family members are. My family members are all over the United States right now. And I know that life will never be the same as it was before. But at least we're alive.

There'll be no more family dinners at Thanksgiving. My niece was trapped in the flood waters while she was pregnant and got a cut on her leg and a terrible infection. Habitat For Humanity just gave her and her three kids a home in Oklahoma City. She's got a home now, a new car; she's not going anywhere.

One of my sisters has moved to Atlanta, Georgia. My mother's in Baton Rogue, and she can't be moved at all anymore. My other sister, who lived with Mom, is looking to live somewhere else. And my brother is in Arkansas. My family is all over the place. And there's no way we can afford to go back to where we were before.

Then there's my mother. The kids are so close to her. And for them to see their grandma's health deteriorating in the midst of this disaster was just so sad. Because life without grandma will never be the same. The kids used to spend every weekend at their grandma's—every weekend. There was just this bond that they had. And life isn't going to be like that anymore. It's hard for them to understand.

We've lost access to our family. We've lost our home and all our possessions. We've lost everything.

But we're rebuilding, here in Texas, bit by bit. And we're making new friends. I mean, being here has been wonderful. Lynn and I have become real friends. We bonded. When Lynn was gone during Rita, we were all freaking out. Daylen was like, "When's Lynn coming back, I miss her."

LYNN: I bet Mariah didn't miss me or my dogs! (*Teasing*) Mariah's a little afraid of dogs.

PATRICE: No, she did!

LYNN: But Daylen missed the dogs, right, Daylen?

DAYLEN BRIANT: I like it here. I like to play with the dogs the most. And I like the pool.

LYNN: He's learning to swim.

PATRICE: Right now we're just trying to return to some kind of normalcy. Last Monday the kids all started school, they're already gettin' into their routines.

As for David and I, well, we're still looking for jobs. I don't know what I'll be able to do. After sleeping in that car for a week, my back problems have gotten worse. So I made a doctor's appointment.

I was on disability back home. And I may have to continue with that, which is fine, because that's my regular income anyway. And David's been sending out résumés everywhere. I know findin' a job is gonna be hard because there are a lot of evacuees here. I think a lot of professional people came towards the Houston area. Who knows how long it'll take? Hopefully not forever.

DAVID: It's very difficult. I'm not used to bein' home, you know! (*Laughs*)

PATRICE: David's crackin' up cause he's just always worked. And then when you can't get a job—it's just tough. And as if it wasn't hard enough to find work already, at every interview you go to, they all want references. Who am I gonna call? There's no city of New Orleans to refer to anymore. You can't call the hotel where I used to work 'cause it's gone. So it may be an uphill battle.

I suppose we'll just stay here with Lynn until she throws us out.

LYNN: Tomorrow! (*Laughter*)

Honestly, I haven't put any time constraints on them. I would just imagine, as anybody would, having your own family, that you would want privacy. I'd imagine that once Patrice and David get jobs, naturally they're gonna want a place of their own. It's not going to be a matter of me throwing them out or them hastily deciding to leave. It's just a matter of a normal family wanting a normal household.

PATRICE: That's definitely what we want. And we're not under any illusions that anyone's gonna make that happen for us but us. I mean, we're getting assistance from FEMA. They just give out a flat $2,000, whether you're an individual or a family of five, like us. I don't think that's fair—one person gets $2,000 and then a family of five gets $2,000?

LYNN: It's not fair.

PATRICE: And Red Cross? After sitting on hold for five hours the first day, the phone cut off. I sat on the phone forever, forever, forever. And sometimes they'd cut you off. And sometimes you'd think you were connected and then it would click over to a message saying that you'd called the wrong number. And then it would tell you to call that same number again. It's just a bunch of crap. People give all that money and their phone system doesn't work during a national crisis?

LYNN: But there are people here in Texas that have just done so much to help. Wednesday we went to the Katy Christian Ministries and we were able to get $75 vouchers for clothes. Then we visited the Food Pantry, where they gave us sacks and sacks and sacks of groceries. I mean, I think the city of Katy and the state of Texas have done more than any of the federal agencies or national charities. The Red Cross and Salvation Army, as far as I'm concerned, have been horrible. We went down to the State of Texas—what was that place called?

PATRICE: The Department of Social Services. And it was weird. In the state of Louisiana, I'd applied for the food card. And they only gave you the food card for one month. Here in Texas, that card gives you three months. What I found amazing was that Texas was doing more for the people from Louisiana than the state of Louisiana was.

Maybe it's the people? I mean, when people see your car has a Louisiana license plate and they're like, "Welcome to Texas. Hope you're findin' everything okay. Hope people treatin' you right." They're just really nice.

We were at the United Way the other day and a woman there just gave me a huge amount of clothes. They were for a relative of hers who had just evacuated from New Orleans, but that relative had since moved on to Chicago, so she asked me "Well, what size do you wear?" I didn't say what size, but I am a large person. I'm not petite. And you don't find a lot of large women's clothing out there for free. They can give you a million dollars worth of vouchers and you can't find it. And this lady had a whole carload of large sizes. She was just a godsend.

We also met the town fire chief at the United Way. And he asks, "You guys from New Orleans?" And we're like, "Yeah." And he says, "Well, go down to the firehouse and tell 'em the chief sent ya." So we go down there and they give us all these Wal-Mart gift cards, worth close to three hundred dollars.

I mean the assistance we've gotten here in Texas is amazing. And, of course, Lynn's the best of the bunch. I can't imagine ever losing touch with her. In fact, I think she would hurt me if I didn't stay in touch! Oh my goodness! (*Laughter*)

LYNN: I'm violent. Very violent.

PATRICE: She would track me down like a dog if I didn't stay in touch. I couldn't imagine where we would be if we hadn't responded to that ad. I just couldn't even imagine. I owe so much to her. Because it's a great school district, it's a safe home. The bus stop for the kids is right outside the house. And Daylen has his dogs! I mean, it's almost like it was meant to happen.

LYNN: Mariah hates the dogs, by the way. (*Laughter*) ⇨

⇨ THE EAST

A HOST LISTING FROM
HURRICANEHOUSING.ORG

I cry every time I watch the devastation caused by Katrina and want to help in a bigger way than just donating money. I am a supervisor in a manufacturing facility in central New York and could assist you in finding a job if you are ready to work. The school systems in the area are fabulous. I can offer you my hand in friendship, a place in my home, and a clean quiet environment. I know this is a long way from your home, whether it was in New Orleans or Mississippi. Sometimes a change in scenery and new friends is just what is needed. I can offer both.

DONNA P.
WEST EDMOND, NEW YORK

"THEY'RE VERY DEDICATED TO THEIR beliefs. I thought it was fascinating, another way to learn about different spiritualities and outlooks and so on."

JENNIFER LINDSAY: When Stephen got accepted at Tulane in the graduate program for Anthropology, we decided to pack up and move down to New Orleans. He's originally from the Gulf Coast, Long Beach, Mississippi—the place that was flattened.

STEPHEN LINDSAY: We actually found an aerial photo of the house in Long Beach that we used to live in, my dad and I, and it's just not there any more.

JENNIFER: We heard that there was an evacuation order coming through. So we packed up the car, a white '95 Ford Taurus with about 80,000 miles on it that my grandmother gave us when we got pregnant. Steven was going to stay behind to board up the house and watch the cats. We have three: Queen, Ooli and Hari. We figured it would just be hot and uncomfortable for a few days because the power was going to go out. Lorien, our two-year-old, and I were going to go visit my grandmother and relatives in Austin.

Well, we got six miles from the house, out onto I-10, and the car died in the 105-degree heat. It just all of a sudden went, right in the middle of traffic, the middle lane. I couldn't even roll the windows down because they were electric. And the traffic was so tight I couldn't even open the doors. I was totally flipping out, because my child was in the backseat, sweat pouring off of him. I couldn't push the car by myself. Finally, this really great Samaritan pulled over, a middle-aged white guy named Glen, I think it was. We tried to jumpstart the battery, but that didn't work. I sat in his SUV with him, his wife and his five children, with my two-year-old for two hours with the air-conditioning on until a tow truck finally came.

We got the car towed six miles back to the house. At that point, it was like six at night. Stephen and another neighbor who'd been evacuated from an offshore oil rig that morning—we'd never even met him before—talked it over and decided that it probably wasn't the battery, it was the alternator. So they hopped in the neighbor's car to go see if they could find someplace to buy an alternator.

STEPHEN: Of course at this point, every place is getting boarded up, and there's not a mechanic to be found anywhere. We went to a Wal-Mart, but they were closed. We found an AutoZone that was still open, even as they were boarding up the windows, and I went in and bought an alternator—paid the two-hundred-fifty bucks—and just hoped that was going to fix it. But by that time, it was too dark to work on the car, and I didn't have tools. Mine were in storage. The next morning, I borrowed a socket set from yet another neighbor and managed to take the old alternator out and put the new one in. I had many moments of doubt.

JENNIFER: Our whole family was freaking out because at that point, we had just told them, "Look, we're going to have to hunker down and ride it out, because we have no way to get dependably out of the city and we don't want to get stuck on the highway in the middle of the storm." Our neighbors had a two-story house. We thought, *Okay, if it gets really bad, we'll go next door with Steve and Lauren.*

It was so freaky. I took Lorien out of the house because I had everything packed. I was like, "We don't need to be underfoot while Daddy's freaking out." We went just down the block. I started to see the storm approaching. The street was really empty and the wind was blowing. We went to a playground first and we were the only ones there. Then we walked in front of one of the Catholic churches. People kept pulling up next to us, saying, "Is there mass? Is there mass?" Finally, somebody came out and said, "Well, there's no mass, but the archbishop is up there kneeling in

[back row, left to right] Giorgia E. (host), Camilla (host's daughter), Lorien Lindsay (evacuee), Stephen Getman (evacuee), Mathias (host's son); [front row, left to right] Theo (host's son), Jennifer Lindsay (evacuee), Anika (host's daughter)

front of the altar if you wanna go join him." Then I walked back across the street and my ears popped from the pressure change, like in an airplane. That's when my stomach dropped. I knew I couldn't cry, because I didn't wanna scare the baby, but I thought, *We're going to die. We're screwed.*

Just then, Stephen called me on the cell phone and said, "I got the car fixed. Come home." So I ran home, five blocks, with the stroller. The poor child was bouncing. We threw the cats in the back seat. We threw Lorien in and as much stuff as we could fit in the car.

It took us over three-and-a-half hours just to get out of the city. And we almost didn't get out. We were on old Route 90, when the local radio station said, "There's something weird happening on Route 90. It's closed off." The Fort Pike drawbridge had been raised and when they shut it, it wouldn't lock, so all the people on 90 trying to evacuate out of the poorer sections and the older sections of town were stuck.

STEPHEN: They wouldn't let them across.

JENNIFER: We ended up wandering the back roads of Mississippi. We got off the big roads as soon as we could because traffic was so crazy. We didn't run the air conditioning because we were afraid the car was going to overheat. We didn't know if the alternator was going to work or not.

STEPHEN: The cats complained the entire time. Lorien didn't say a word. I made sure we'd grabbed whatever portable food we had.

JENNIFER: We were living on peanut butter crackers.

STEPHEN: I was concerned that we might get stuck, and there was no telling how long we were going to be in the car, and so I made sure that we had food and water. We didn't stop for anything but gas. It took us eighteen hours to get to my parents' house in Arkansas. We left at twelve-thirty in the afternoon, and we arrived at six-thirty the next morning. It's usually about an eight- or nine-hour trip.

We ended up staying in Arkansas for around two weeks. We were completely in limbo for a while and we didn't know where to look for housing, because we didn't know where we were going to end up going.

JENNIFER: And then the Smithsonian posted this great email offer of fellowships for displaced graduate students to come to D.C.

STEPHEN: And I said, "Wow, sign me up."

JENNIFER: We've both lived in D.C. before. But the only way we could do the D.C. option was if we could find low-cost or free housing, because I knew how expensive it was here. And then, at the HurricaneHousing website, I found Giorgia.

Giorgia called Stephen's parents' house and said, "So, you're coming." I said, "Well, we have the cats." And she said, "Well, we have dogs. Is that a problem?" And I said, "No, because the cats are outdoor cats." She said, "Okay, fine. But we also have kids. It's kind of noisy." And I said, "Well, we have a small child—he's pretty noisy, too."

GIORGIA E. MATHIAS: We are extremely noisy. My oldest daughter, Camilla, and my son Mathias are both ten. Theo is six years old and Anika's four. All our kids play instruments, including drums, and they practice every morning before school. That's the only way that I can make sure they practice every day, because after school, they have homework. I apologized and said I was sorry but I just couldn't change the system because it worked for me. They were totally cool with that.

JENNIFER: I told her we'd take it. We packed up the car and drove out here. They were so welcoming and so sweet. Theo and Anika made us little cards when we got here that said, "Welcome to your new home. Happy you live here." It made me cry. We put them on the refrigerator, so we had refrigerator art to start off with. Lorien and Theo fell in love with each other, so it was a good fit.

It's been really strange though I gotta admit, because we haven't really had a home for a while. We've just been living out of our suitcases.

GIORGIA: Christian, my husband, is an economist. He works for the World Bank and he's always traveling. It was his idea to offer to help. At first, I didn't understand the magnitude of what had happened with Katrina. But we'd been pretty touched by the tsunami. We'd been away on vacation when the tsunami hit, and we had to cut the vacation short so that he could go down to the Maldives.

He basically spent the rest of the year trying to help the government come up with a strategy to use the money they're borrowing from the World Bank to get back on their feet. We were just having lunch, maybe five, six days after Katrina, and he said, "We should really invite a family to stay with us." And I said, "Yeah, that's a good idea." There was no discussion.

It's been great. The kids love it, particularly Theo—he loves to have Lorien here. The basement is a self-sufficient apartment, so that we can all have independence if we want it, and then hang out when we want to.

Actually, having other adults around the house is nice. They've been super. Whenever they saw that something needed to be done, they just did it. My dog kept digging the gravel out of the backyard, onto the path, and they would just clean it up. There was a leak upstairs with the faucet and Stephen came up and fixed it. He fixed the lock on the door too.

JENNIFER: They feel more like long-term friends than strangers. It's funny, because I've always had these ideals of having this kind of group house. I've lived in group houses before, I know it's not really that fun. But I had this image, when we moved down to New Orleans, of having a duplex and having a good relationship with whoever our tenants were, swapping childcare and borrowing cups of sugar. And we had a lot of that going on. Everybody composted. Everybody did recycling. We all had the same kind of mentality. To come to a household that does all that just reinforces my hopes.

GIORGIA: We are very compatible, even though they're very different, in terms of spiritual beliefs and so on. Chris is not in any way religious. I was raised Catholic but I've sort of been wandering between various religions. Niff and Stephen are pagan naturalists. I never knew any pagan naturalists before. They're very dedicated to their beliefs. I thought it was fascinating, another way to learn about different spiritualities and outlooks and so on. I think maybe it came up when I asked them if they celebrated Christmas. They didn't, but they celebrate all sorts of other holi-

days, like the winter solstice. I was interested, so Stephen ordered a book from Amazon for me to read about it.

JENNIFER: We got her *Drawing Down the Moon* by Margot Adler. It's a great introductory book to paganism.

GIORGIA: I'm sure Theo had plenty of questions. He's never hesitated to ask questions.

JENNIFER: I've taken some of the kids to the playground and Giorgia's watched Lorien a couple times. We've made dinner together twice and the kids have watched movies together. Lorien loves it. He was miserable in Arkansas, because it's a retirement community, so there were no kids there. Here, he sits at the top of stairs and says, "Kids? Upstairs, kids! Kids here?" I've been taking him out to all the playgrounds and I've made friends with some of the other moms and some of the nannies in the neighborhood. The coolest thing is that Giorgia speaks Italian to the kids and Christian speaks German to the kids, so they're growing up with three languages. I'm hoping Lorien will pick up some of those.

I'm still a new mother. And I think we've become better parents from watching Giorgia and Christian. It totally changed the way we parented and added tools we didn't have. Her house is completely kid-focused. Each kid has his own room and each room has special things in it for the kids. They go out as a couple too, but they primarily do things with their kids. They got season tickets to the Shakespeare Festival and they'd take one kid with them and get a sitter for the others. The kid would get to have one-on-one time with both parents and get to go see Shakespeare. They just have this total involvement with their children.

STEPHEN: The plan is for us to go back in December. But who knows what the infrastructure is going to be.

GIORGIA: We'll just kind of see what happens.

JENNIFER: We've already told Giorgia and Christian they have to come down to New Orleans once we get settled.

STEPHEN: Or when a hurricane hits Washington, D.C.

JENNIFER: If you guys have a blizzard, you can come down and visit us where it's nice and warm. ⇨

"**YOU JUST ASK PEOPLE WHAT THEY need. 'How can I help you?' Every day, if you can."**

PATRIZIA CIOFFI: I'm a voice teacher and a classical singer. A soprano. I work at several adult schools, and I do volunteer work. I also do a lot of concerts. Classical, jazz, pop—I have a fairly broad repertory. Right now, I'm working for various organizations and churches that produce music programs.

I've been in this house about thirty-seven years. I was born in Bloomfield in a middle-class Italian family, but I grew up in Glen Ridge, which is about a block away from here. I have four bedrooms and after my kids left and got married or went to college, I started renting a room. I have space in the house and I like to share it.

Often, I've rented to women who were either getting a divorce or regrouping their lives or who'd just come out of an illness. Usually on a whatever-they-can-afford basis. I also had a student living here for thirteen years, a Yugoslavian-American opera student named Iris, who was terribly disappointed with the big schools in New York City. So we engaged in the old classical training method where she lived with her teacher and sang every day. She was moving, the month after Sena moved in, so it worked out really well.

I have two pianos, and when I'm teaching, sometimes people come and rehearse upstairs. I like to offer parts of the house that aren't being used to young students who need a place that's comfortable and quiet. It's relatively quiet, right? It's not too noisy?

SENA AGBLEY: Yeah.

PATRIZIA: When Katrina happened, I thought, *Well, I don't have a lot of money. What do I have to give? I have space.* I didn't want to call the Red Cross, because I know there's all kinds of red tape. My son-in-law said MoveOn.org was

expediting housing, so I went online and I registered. I listed it three times to make sure that I didn't mess up. (*Laughter*)

I'm not that savvy on the computer. I actually got two responses and the second one contacted me twice. Then Sena, maybe a week after the crisis hit. He said, "I need to rent a space or get a room." I said, "You don't have to pay." But he said he wanted to, so we worked out something he could afford. I gave him the small room, because the big room's occupied, and had an electrician put in some outlets by his desk to make the room more student-friendly. And it's worked out. Usually I don't rent to two people, but I was prepared to give up that room under any circumstances, either with someone paying or not paying.

SENA: I pay about half the rent. I'm originally from Ghana in West Africa, the eastern Volta region. My mom is a teacher and a school administrator and my dad is a civil servant. I got my Bachelor's in mining engineering in Ghana and I went to Kiel, Germany to do my Masters in coastal geology. I'm currently studying—I *was* studying—at Tulane University. Before the storm, I was doing a doctorate program in environmental science. I had been there for one year.

I lived alone in East New Orleans, on the first floor. I left New Orleans on Sunday. On Saturday evening, the mayor said he was calling a mandatory evacuation. Most people knew what would happen if a big storm hit New Orleans because of the river, the lake and all the canals. So when they said the storm was pretty much directed toward New Orleans, it was a good idea to leave. I decided to come to New Jersey, because I have an uncle in East Orange. I took a flight.

I stayed with my uncle one week. After the first few days, it was clear that my school was gonna be closed for the semester. Tulane encouraged its students to take classes for the fall in whatever university you could find. I decided to complete my fall semester at Montclair State.

[left to right] Patrizia Cioffi (host), Sena Agbley (evacuee)

Because of the hurricane situation, they made it quite easy to transfer. I've got a full scholarship at Tulane and Montclair gave me the same offer. They pay my tuition and I get support also for my research assistantship. They give me a stipend every two weeks.

When I got admission at Montclair, I decided to find accommodation closer to campus. On Craigslist, I saw a link for HurricaneHousing.org. I saw a lot of posts, but I wrote to only Patrizia. She said she was willing to take in one person and most of the other ads said they were willing to take in four or five. I didn't want to get crowded in the house and also, I have to study.

PATRIZIA: I really don't like too many people in the house. I like a peaceful house. Too many people needing the bathroom or needing the kitchen; it's hard on them. But I like guests in my house. It's a lot of space for one person.

I work a lot, so I don't go out much, but I try to make a couple dinners a week. And if I don't have a formal dinner, I leave it on the stove for him. He's very independent, and our schedules are…he's out late, and I'm home teaching, which is good because he doesn't have to listen to it. The walls are pretty good though, aren't they? The plaster walls are thick. It doesn't disturb you.

SENA: No, it doesn't disturb me. And she has been so nice, helping me settle down, doing groceries. She got me a bicycle. Stuff like that. We went to the theater. We saw *Pippin*. It was nice.

PATRIZIA: It was community theatre. Two of my students were in it. If things come up, I'll invite him to go with me. I said to him, "I'm a really busy person, so just make this your home, and if you need anything, just ask me."

Sena's really good with the dog. I have a black and white shi'tzu poodle named Marcello who's seven years old and adorable. He'll say, "Do you want me to walk the dog?" At ten o'clock at night, when I'm exhausted, he'll actually offer to walk the dog! So that's a big help. And

he takes the garbage out every Wednesday and Thursday nights. I hate taking out the garbage. (*Laughter*)

But Sena is very quiet, in his room a lot. He studies quite a bit.

SENA: I'm gonna be here until December or January. I lost what I couldn't take along. I brought with me only a small bag full of clothes. Nobody was expecting the worse-case scenario, so I just took what I needed for two or three days.

PATRIZIA: I got a thing from MoveOn before Sena came, a letter of agreement they said that people should use because some people were encountering problems. Or they implied that some people might be encountering problems. That was a cumbersome thing to consider.

I'm very lucky. I have a student who's a serious student and not someone who's out in the street without any focus or life. I have wondered how it would have been for me, had I taken in very poor people who had nothing, which I was prepared to do. Sending out the message, "Please come live in my house"…honestly, has really been a gift *to me*. Now I'm thinking maybe I ought to reopen another gift when he leaves and offer his room to somebody else who needs a place.

You just ask people what they need. "How can I help you?" Every day, if you can. Obviously, Sena is so together a person that I don't need to ask him, I don't think. He'll ask me if he needs a ride or whatever, but it must be difficult. He's got this sense of integrity that's very strong. I've been lucky. It comes with the kind of person that he is. Pursuing his studies, he's very diligent. He's that way in all the things he does. He's from a city in Ghana, a very busy city, and he's very cosmopolitan, you know. He's cool. He's not a farm boy. Some people talk to him and they don't realize how sophisticated he is because he's so quiet.

He's hip. He knows what's going on. ⇨

NORMAN BROWN: Participating in the HurricaneHousing program has been a rewarding experience. It's a way to share some of my fortunate meager resources with someone less fortunate. It just feels like the right thing to do. Helping this way has made me more aware of my ability to suppress and change my own desires and needs—my selfishness in other words. It's so meaningful to me because I know I'm providing a safe and nurturing place where Sandra and her daughter can begin healing from the disaster and the losses it caused. I feel good that she has the support she needs to start their lives again. ⇨

[left to right] Norman Brown (host), Sandra McDonald

"**B**OTH MY FAMILY AND DIANA'S are Creole, so the bloodline runs pretty deep. My grandmother still speaks Creole French. She grew up on a plantation in rural Louisiana. Her maiden name is Baptiste. The Blache name goes back to Marseille, France. That's why we named our daughter Marseille."

DIANA BLACHE: We were high school sweethearts, me and Gus. We've been together ever since. We were both raised in the New Orleans area.

GUSTAVE BLACHE III: We actually met in junior high school. We started dating in high school. And at the time, I was also going to an art school. I'm a painter—a figurative painter, kind of in the style of the great French and Spanish impressionists like Degas and Velasquez. My work shows in New York and in New Orleans, where I still have a gallery representing me.

DIANA: Gus has been doing his artwork since we first met. We moved up to New York the first time right after we got married, so he could study painting in graduate school.

GUSTAVE: That's where they beat me over the head with the whole 19th century art influence. I was really drawn to it on my own though. And coming from New Orleans, I guess, subconsciously, that style might already have seeped into my head. I mean, they had a Degas museum there that I always used to go to as a kid. And my instructor in high school, he was really into the whole turn-of-the-century Ashcan School, which had a big influence on a lot of Creole painters in New Orleans.

DIANA: If you're from New Orleans, that kinda thing gets in your bones. When I discovered I was pregnant, after we'd been living in New York for around four years, I just immediately thought it was time to go back. The New Orleans area was the center of our family—all our traditions. We could get help with the baby from our relatives. And it's got just a slower pace to raise a child.

GUSTAVE: We thought it would be cool for our daughter to get a feel for the Creole culture that we were steeped in as kids. Both my family and Diana's are Creole, so the bloodline runs pretty deep. My grandmother still speaks Creole French. She grew up on a plantation in rural Louisiana. Her maiden name is Baptiste. The Blache name goes back to Marseille, France. That's why we named our daughter Marseille.

DIANA: And where we were living—in the Garden District— it's totally steeped in history. Before Katrina came, it just seemed like the coolest place for a kid to grow up.

GUSTAVE: But unfortunately, I don't think that's gonna happen now. Don't think we'll be going back any time soon. 'Cause our house was basically ruined. We're in New York now. I have a job here. I think we have to...just start our life over.

There'd be a lot of things that would have to happen in New Orleans before we'd consider going back. I mean, having to evacuate every two months for a hurricane is just not how we wanna live our lives anymore. Even before Katrina, we were getting fed up with that aspect. And now, there's no telling how long it'll take to get the levees fixed and the economy back in line. To be honest, I'd actually feel better if the rest of my extended family left too.

DIANA: When the hurricane hit, we chose to evacuate with Gustave's mother and her parents to Deridder, Louisiana. We stayed there for two weeks before realizing we had nothing to go back to. So we started trying to make plans for where we could possibly go to make money, where we

[left to right] Diana Blache (evacuee), Gustave Blache III (evacuee), Marseille Blache (evacuee), Blerti Murataj (host), Beth Cloutier (host)

could find housing, anything of that sort. 'Cause Gus was, like, really itchy. Stir-crazy.

GUSTAVE: You go hang around Deridder for two weeks. See how you like it.

DIANA: Gustave always painted from home. He had a full-time job but he painted nights and weekends. We had a studio set up in the house for him. So leaving New Orleans, he left his studio, his supplies, his paintings, everything. It was...

GUSTAVE: It sucked.

DIANA: (*Laughs*) Yeah. Our idea was maybe to go to Dallas—where most of my family evacuated—or to Chicago, where we had relatives, or to Baton Rouge, which was just close. So I started searching. We were using the Internet at the library in Deridder and I just happened upon HurricaneHousing through Craigslist. There were places in New York, kind of near to where we used to live. And I thought,

Well, if we could find a job in New York, we'll go back. We'll at least give it a shot.

GUSTAVE: A lot of old friends from graduate school reached out to me. And I was like, "Well, if you know of any job opportunities..." It ended up that there was an opening at a restoration place, restoring old 19th century master works. And once I got the offer...

DIANA: We just decided to move. So I submitted the application to HurricaneHousing and we started getting calls back from different people. A lot of them were offering their couch and things like that. But we're a family with a newborn, so we were looking, ideally, for an actual vacant apartment. And then we met Beth.

BETH CLOUTIER: That's me! (*Laughs*) I lived in Hoboken, New Jersey, but I recently moved into Midtown Manhattan with Blerti, my fiancé.

BLERTI MURATAJ: Okay. Hi. Originally I'm from Albania.

DIANA: These guys are the best. You should be writing the book about them.

BLERTI: No. Oh no.

DIANA: Tell the story! (*Laughs*)

BETH: Well, it's pretty simple. We were watching the news and I was just fed up with what I was seeing, what was happening in Louisiana and the slow response that our government was having down there. And when I received MoveOn.org's email looking for housing for victims, I wanted to help somebody. So I talked to Blerti and we discussed it. We planned on moving in together in early October and I decided because of the hurricane that, if it was okay with him, I would move to his place a month early and give my place up to house some people. And he was totally fine with it. So I just posted something immediately: "I have a two-bedroom, full kitchen, bath, living room to offer in Hoboken, New Jersey and it will be fully paid. You're not gonna have to pay expenses or rent for a month."

GUSTAVE: Good deal, eh?

BETH: In the past so many good things have been done for me by people who didn't necessarily know me very well. And I felt that it was a good opportunity to give back. And when I spoke with Diana, I kind of went on my gut feeling...

GUSTAVE: It seemed kind of meant to be, in a way.

DIANA: From the time we talked over the phone, they were just very welcoming. They even picked us from the airport, which we knew was a luxury in New York. They showed us around, tried to get us acclimated to the area, took us out to dinner. They were just really helpful and constantly bringing stuff to us that people had donated, clothing and...

GUSTAVE: Yeah, baby clothes.

DIANA: They just went above and beyond. We definitely have lifelong friends from this. Definitely. They're our kind of people. Just really down to earth, really sweet, helpful people. And like I told them I can't wait 'til I have my own place so I can have them over for dinner.

GUSTAVE: I know. I know.

BLERTI: Okay. We'll come. (*Laughter*)

GUSTAVE: We actually went to the same college too. Even graduated around the same time.

BETH: When Diana emailed me, she said, "Oh, check out my husband's artwork." And when I researched it online, I saw that he graduated from SVA, School of Visual Arts. And I was like, "Hey, I went to the School of Visual Arts." And so we started talking and we were like, "Do you know so-and-so? Do you know so-and-so?" And we just totally clicked, totally clicked.

BLERTI: I went to SVA too.

GUSTAVE: Party!

BLERTI: Exactly.

BETH: SVA, man!

DIANA: Instant connection.

BETH: I feel like we've known them for ages. It's kind of one of those bizarre distant friendships where you come together and you're like, "Hey, what's going on?" You slap and hands and you're like, "Let's go have a beer." It's very relaxed and it's very good.

BLERTI: They are such optimistic people. They never get down because of their situation. Even when they're going through this hardship, they still smile and hope.

DIANA: Before Beth and Blerti gave us a place to stay, the three of us were living with twelve other people in a two-bedroom. ...

GUSTAVE: Yeah. (*Laughs*) I mean, it's weird looking back. Because we ended up being pretty lucky. And I'm totally, totally grateful. But, at the same time, I don't feel like an optimist. I mean, you know, it's difficult.

DIANA: Yeah, no, that's true.

GUSTAVE: I guess what we've gone through in terms of relocating has been, I would say, just the state of limbo—not having stability, not knowing where we're gonna be the next week or the week after. I like to have a stable home environment for my daughter. I mean, your home should be a haven. You don't realize how valuable your comfort zone can be—to know where the light switch is in the bathroom, how to flush your toilet so the water doesn't run. (*Laughs*) We don't have that now. And as a result, our weekends—the only time we have off from our jobs—are all about shopping and trying to find our next place to live.

We lost our van in the floods, so we haven't had our own transportation. When we're finally able get a car, we'll be able to have a bit more of a life—maybe some socializing, going out to eat, being able to have a glass of wine, relax a little bit. If you can't do that in this city, New York really loses its appeal. It becomes stress on top of stress.

DIANA: It is strange to feel so rootless. I mean, both of our parents lost their homes completely. Typically, if something happens at your house, you might go to Mom's. Well, Mom's house is gone too, so...

GUSTAVE: We lost quite a bit. I had been storing pretty much all of my old paintings at my mom's house. When we left, I was only able to take three with me. So I lost roughly thirty pieces, not counting the ones that were in progress at my studio. And a lot of the pieces at my mom's were college paintings—studies. They kind of represented a growth period. My pictures sell for pretty decent prices these days. So, at some point, later in my career, those paintings could've had a pretty decent value. But more than anything, they had a personal value. I won't be able to look back and see my transition now. I can remember it but it's not the same. It's a loss of my memories. The same with my mother's house itself. We *grew up* at my mother's home.

DIANA: My mother's house is full of mold. It had only like a foot of water. But there was mold up to the roof. And so it's likely most things won't be salvaged—childhood pictures and all the other little things that were sentimental to us.

GUSTAVE: We saw my mother's house on the Internet and it was flooded to the roof. There were boats driving past it. It's just a loss. We'll be going back to make sure, of course. If I have any supplies or pictures and clothes, winter clothes, I would still love to retrieve them. But I don't...

DIANA: It's where our family comes from. That was the main reason we wanted to stay living in New Orleans, so our child could know our families. I wanted her to grow up with a sense our history, you know? Like a place you belong to. And that's all gone. It's hard.

GUSTAVE: We even had a baby room set up for Marseille at my mom's house. We'd bring her there every weekend and spend time with our families—both sets of grandparents. We'd go get crawfish and shrimp and boil 'em and hang out.

But now, everyone's dispersed. We actually just spent Christmas in Dallas. Diana's family relocated there. So we got a chance to hang with her family. But there wasn't that sense of feeling at home for the holidays. Everyone was still getting acclimated. Even when we lived in New York before, we'd go back to New Orleans every year for Christmas. So this year it was difficult.

One of my oldest friends, she used to live a couple blocks away from my mom's house. And every day before Christmas—I'm terrible at wrapping presents—I'd go to her house and she'd wrap all my Christmas presents for me. So for the past, like, fifteen years, it was kind of a tradition. If my friend wasn't in town, her *mother* would do it for me. (*Laughs*) So I talked to that friend this year on Christmas. She'd gone to Baton Rouge, where her mom had relocated. And apparently, they were sittin' around, reminiscin' and her mom said, "Wouldn't it be funny if Gus knocked on our door right now and asked us to wrap his gifts?" It was first time I wasn't able to spend that time with them in fifteen years.

I miss that sense of family. But hopefully we'll be able to find it some time again, here in New York. Once we get past the bare necessities, it'll be easier to think about other stuff. We'll just be able to enjoy New York more. We're not enjoying anything at the moment. But I think once we have, like, a sofa to sit on, that'll change things quite a bit.

DIANA: I think that'll do it.

GUSTAVE: Yeah. ⇨

A helicopter flies over flooded New Orleans.

**RYNELL TAYLOR
& JASMINE BLANEY
KRISTOFF CHAMONIKLOLAS**

NEW YORK, NEW YORK

**VIVIAN TARTTER
ALEXANDER TARTTER**

"ANOTHER PERSON WOULD BE LIKE, 'I'm not going to let them people in. Will they steal from me? Will they do this?' It's good to know that in this cold-hearted world, there's still good people. It makes me feel much, much better."

JASMINE BLANEY: Me and Rynell lived in the uptown area of New Orleans. I'm from Alabama and I was a last-semester graduating college student from Xavier University. I'm an accounting major.

RYNELL TAYLOR: I was working at the Housing Authority, taking care of the office area and different properties around the city. I lived in New Orleans my whole life. We actually got married February 1ˢᵗ of this year.

VICKY TARTTER: You're still newlyweds.

JASMINE: We're young, but we've known each other since 2003.

RYNELL: I met her when I was working as a cashier in a restaurant. She just walked in and I decided to talk to her and we kicked it for a little bit. It was a pretty simple wedding. We went to City Hall and got it done.

VICKY: Hell of a honeymoon.

JASMINE: The Saturday before we evacuated, I'd bought a bus ticket so we could go back to Alabama. I bought the bus ticket and twenty minutes later, they cancelled the bus—they closed the bus station, so I left with a friend, in a car. But I left Rynell and the rabbit. I had a rabbit that I got for my twenty-first birthday. His name was David Wellington.

RYNELL: The rabbit's name was Pookie.

JASMINE: That's what I *call* him!

RYNELL: David Wellington! (*Laughs*) That rabbit's name was Pookie!

JASMINE: Victor Saint David Wellington is his real name. He's a dwarf. Really sweet. To me, he was a little person. Like, he would turn off the alarm clock if I didn't hit it fast enough. Turn the TV channels...

VICKY: He turned the TV channels?

JASMINE: Yeah. He's able to stand on his hind legs and just kick the channels. He didn't like cartoons.

RYNELL: He turned the TV channels, ate regular food...

JASMINE: He was just cool. I left him because my friend only had enough space for me and a small bag, and we'd only anticipated being gone a couple of days. When I left, the storm had just crossed over Florida and it was still a Category One. As we were driving, it got worse. We were in Mississippi when the levees broke, so we really didn't have time to anticipate.

RYNELL: Right as we were stuck in the really long traffic lines, trying to get out of the state, that's when they issued a mandatory evacuation. That's when I realized I should have taken the rabbit. I drove to Jackson, Mississippi and then to my friend's family in Eatonton, Georgia. Stayed there for like two weeks, until I came up here to meet Jasmine by bus.

Long bus ride.

KRISTOFF CHAMONIKOLAS: I'm originally from the Czech Republic and I am a graduate student at Charles University in Prague. I came to New Orleans as an international student at the University of New Orleans. I'd spent twelve days in New Orleans before the hurricane came. I study English and American Studies and I'm writing my Masters thesis on American politics. I got out of the town about twenty-four hours before the landfall. I was traveling with a group of fourteen international students.

When I came to New York, for the first two or three weeks, I was staying with a friend of mine who had a tiny apartment in East Village. She's getting married and mov-

[back row, left to right] Rynell Taylor (evacuee), Jasmine Blaney (evacuee), Vivian Tartter (host); [front row, left to right] Alexander Tartter (host's son), Kristoff Chamonikolas (evacuee)

ing out of her apartment, so I wasn't able to stay there for any longer. I met another international student refugee from New Orleans at Columbia and she told me about HurricaneHousing.org.

VICKY: I'm a professor of psychology at City College, where I direct the Masters program. I teach experimental psychology, cognitive psychology, the psychology of language and memory. Not anything socially useful. (*Laughter*)

I live with my two sons, Xander and Eric, who's a sophomore at SUNY Binghamton and had left a room behind. I had both a spare bedroom that's reasonably large and a guest room. I asked Eric if he had a problem with his room being used and it was quite the contrary, under the circumstances.

I was appalled, as I think most of the world was, at the tremendous failure of government response and then the quibbling when things needed to be done. And I had all

this extra space. From the moment the levees had broken, I started to say to friends, I can shelter people. I just had no idea of how to get to people to shelter them.

I called Hillary Clinton's office and they gave me the names of a couple of people, but nobody had yet thought about this at the government level. They had a list of parishes, which, I discovered, means something different than what I thought it meant. It means county, not church, but I thought, *great, I'm going to be talking to a deacon, and he'll be able to do the screening*. I called the parishes, thinking it was a church, and got a recording and left a message, and didn't hear back from anyone. But of course, as I kept saying, they were swamped, both physically and literally. I finally got on MoveOn.org. I checked with Xander before I listed and said this was something I wanted to do, because it was clearly going to impact on his life, and was that okay?

ALEXANDER TARTTER: I didn't think it was zany. She said something that I absolutely agree with—that donating money to the Red Cross, or any of these other organizations, doesn't necessarily go to the people who are affected. A percentage of it will go to people who work for the Red Cross, which is okay, they need that. But if she provides a shelter for refugees from New Orleans, that's directly helping these people.

I'm also a very social person, so I like to socialize. We have a good time, watching the Yankee game or whatever's on. It's also very nice to have a foreign person here, because he learned British English, so we had this huge conversation about differences between American English and British English and the spelling and some of the words and different things, which is very interesting to me.

JASMINE: I made the contact with HurricaneHousing.org. I actually found it at HUD.gov and went to the link. You looked for a posting and then you just responded to email.

VICKY: When I advertised the rooms, I pictured a couple staying with their child. I thought there were going to be a lot of people able to find housing, but keeping families together was going to be very tough. The big problem was the Web access. The people who were really needy didn't have Web access.

Jasmine came over in the afternoon and was sort of anxiously expectant, in a job-interview mode. She was friendly and polite and very sweet and a little nervous, but you could say the same thing about me. Kristoff was very open and kind of bouncy. We were eating dinner when he came and I invited him to sit down and have dessert with us. Rynell came a week after I met Jasmine. Rynell was very circumspect and respectful. Jasmine did all the talking.

RYNELL: My first impression of Vicky was that she was an open-minded person who decided to help out the best way she could, instead of just giving money. Vicky's welcomed us with open arms. It's definitely like a family.

One challenge has been the lack of transportation. And learning the city, that's a big challenge. Manhattan is very different. I must be honest. People look at me as if... I don't think it's some race thing, but they obviously look at me. Not stare at me but just glance at me. Maybe because I am a very big person. I'm 6' 3", weight maybe 280. It's different from anything I'd previously experienced.

JASMINE: I still have to go back to New Orleans to graduate, and to figure out some school stuff. Right now, I'm going to St. John's. They have a matriculation agreement with my school, so I was able to go free—books, tuition. They even loaned me a laptop, so that was really great. We're looking into whether New York is going to be an option, but a lot of things are still up in the air, as far as permanent relocation. It hasn't been too bad here, though. We have our own space, so it's not like in the dorms, where there's bathroom lines around the corner. We are all on different schedules, like ships passing in the night.

VICKY: Jasmine spends half the week at St. Johns, in classes all day. I'm older and I get up around ten and go to bed around ten-thirty. They get up, depending on what they have to do, between noon and four and they're up all night. They're on what I would call teenage hours, so they might be having breakfast just before I'd start cooking dinner.

KRISTOFF: I think the difference between me and Rynell and Jasmine is probably that there's no home in New Orleans which I was leaving behind. There's just my dormitory room, where there's still part of my belongings, but I didn't lose anything or anyone. In a way, I'm just doing my research here in New York instead of in New Orleans, and I'm enjoying New York instead of enjoying New Orleans. The main campus of the university was actually one of the highest places in town, so it wasn't severely damaged. They'll almost certainly reopen for classes next semester.

JASMINE: At the apartment complex where we were living, they said the bottom floors were pretty much destroyed. We lived on the second floor, so the waters reached up and came underneath the door, so basically the rug is destroyed but not necessarily stuff that was higher up, like maybe the TV and dressers. They haven't really been in the apartment, though I guess they had to go in the apartment to find my rabbit. About two weeks ago, Rynell told me to go to PetFinder.com. I registered him, told them what he looked like, and I said if you come into the apartment and he doesn't know you, he's going to go underneath the bed. They found him and I saw him online today. I'm very happy about that.

RYNELL: Very happy about that.

VICKY: I didn't know you could do this PetFinders thing that everybody was sharing. One of the things that I think is really cool is the enormous amount of networking. Lots of really, really good grassroots networking among the refugees. The other thing I want to say is that, from Jasmine's point of view, New York really had it together. There were food stamp programs and they were initially given medical care through Medicaid. Refugees went to the outreach and there were clothes there for them to take. The city had it all in one location. It was almost the only thing that was ever done efficiently in a bureaucracy.

JASMINE: I have friends who stayed in Louisiana or went to northern Louisiana and others who went to Texas, and it was just chaos. The Disaster Assistance Service center, where all the programs are set up here, was just beautiful. They gave you ID, and if you lost your ID, they credentialized you. Then they set up an appointment for you and they walked you through every agency imaginable, from FEMA all the way down to the Red Cross, the Salvation Army, DMV. The city organized this. The Office of Emergency Management.

RYNELL: We passed the information on to Kristoff and he did the same exact thing, so it was really great.

VICKY: The cultural differences haven't been an issue. We talk about it a lot. We talk politics. We talk about everybody's beliefs. Rynell is violently against abortion. I am violently pro-choice, but we didn't get violent. He just looked at me sort of startled, thinking, *How could a kind human being feel this way?* And I looked at him startled, thinking, *How could an intelligent human feel that way?* I wish Congress could do so well. We're all humanitarians, I guess. I'm of Jewish extraction, but I don't practice. I feel stupid saying this, but I feel so deeply spiritual, having these people stay with me, all of us surviving. I mean, I didn't survive anything, but I sort of feel like we all survived and we've come together and we've formed a family, and I want to thank the God I don't believe in.

KRISTOFF: It came together really good.

VICKY: We haven't done things together, mostly because of schedules. By the time they get up, I'm ready to go to bed. But they go out. Rynell and Jasmine went to the Philharmonic. Kristoff went to the Metropolitan, to the Czech exhibit. I belong to almost every museum in the city and that gets us free admission.

For Rynell, more than anybody, it's going to be a total change in the direction of life as he'd seen it. He's either hiding it really well or coping really well, but I think it's the most profound thing. His whole life was going to be in New Orleans, with his family, and probably now it's not.

RYNELL: I already have family members saying that they're not going back, so it's really rough. My whole family's all scattered out. So it's really hard. It really is.

JASMINE: It's more or less knowing nothing. Today I called FEMA. They have to assign you an inspector to determine your property loss value. I gave them a couple of weeks and they still haven't done it, but now I have to go and sign up for my apartment—either that or pay rent, and I can't do that. But they haven't assigned me an inspector and there's no way to get reimbursed without it. We have a little grudge going against them.

RYNELL: She has to fly back to New Orleans for a day and she can't stay anywhere and there's no ticket for her to come back, and then she's forced to stay in a hotel and there's no hotel in New Orleans, so she either has to go across the river, and you have to call somebody who has a motor vehicle because there are no taxis, there are no buses or nothing. It's very unfair.

KRISTOFF: I can see one difference between how you handle emergency situations here and how we do that in Europe. I really appreciate the good network of non-governmental agencies and organizers you have here. In Europe, we pay much higher taxes than you do here, which means that if there's a national crisis or even if someone is experiencing a personal crisis, they take it for granted that the state is supposed to take care of everything. We have good social services, free health care and everything, but sometimes it fails, and then the network is not as good or as diverse. Here there are NGOs that can step in and help out when the government—*if* the government fails. I started noticing this during the evacuation. On the way from Louisiana to Mississippi and Arkansas, in almost every small town, there was a sign that the local authority or the local church was setting up a shelter. It was no office doing this. It was just the local communities.

VICKY: Jasmine has health insurance in Louisiana, some sort of HMO, so she's allowed to see a doctor in the Louisiana tri-state area, which didn't quite work in New York. Kristoff, the poor international, has free health insurance for the entire EU.

KRISTOFF: No—the whole world.

VICKY: Free! So when all of them came up here, Kristoff was the only one who came with health insurance. The other difference was that I had to show him how to cash a check. He had to open a bank account, but in the EU everything is done electronically. He was getting a paycheck from Columbia, but he needed to learn how to deposit it. He was very cute about it, but it was very funny.

I've been getting more out of this than I'm giving. I'm getting my empty nest refilled. I feel like our lives have intersected and that somehow this was intended to be. The big thing I feel I'm giving them is an opportunity to consider what they want without feeling threatened, and to deal with the tragedy in a sort of womb-like place where they can figure out where to go from here, without feeling pushed into making a more impulsive or wrong decision.

RYNELL: I just have one more thing to say. Not to bring it into a race thing, but the devastation that was going on, on TV and everything—it looked like predominantly black poor people that was robbing, that was breaking into sports stores, breaking into clothes store. It's just good to see that there are still good people in this world who welcome us with open arms, even after seeing that on TV. When you see something like that, another person might think, "I'm not going to let them people in. Will they steal from me? Will they do this?" It's good to know that in this cold-hearted world, there's still good people. It makes me feel much, much better.

JASMINE: Because she really didn't ask us very intense questions. She asked me a little more about the school: "Where are you at? What do you need help with?" Then she said, "This is what I have to offer. Will that benefit you?" And we worked from there. It wasn't a survey. She didn't have like ten questions you had to fill out, where if you answered yes to this, you can't come, or if you answered no to this, you can't come. I thought that was real generous also.

KRISTOFF: Vicky was also the only volunteer who was willing to take a guy. All the other people only wanted kids or females.

VICKY: Well, you know, Alexander's a second-degree black belt. (*Laughter*)

JASMINE: Built-in security! ⇨

"**E**VERYWHERE YOU LOOK THERE'S a potential heartbreak and that's a negotiation, too. How much heartbreak do you try to avoid and how much do you meet on its own terms?"

ESQUIZITO PEREZ: My home is 1018 Music Street, New Orleans, Louisiana. Yes, I live on Music Street. In the Marigny, which is almost the Bywater. Almost is a very important word in New Orleans. I've lived in my home for approximately seven years. I'm a musician, a jazz vocalist and guitarist. I left New Orleans on Sunday, August 28th.

I woke up that morning with the decision to stay in New Orleans and ride out the storm, as I have many other storms. But they had reports that they were expecting twenty-foot tidal surges and that was my cue to find other options. At best, the levees are twenty feet. Some of them are fifteen. So I figured if they were right about those twenty-foot tidal surges, there would be water. My home has two rooms upstairs, so it would not have been critical, but it would not have been fun. I had an opportunity to leave with some other musicians, so I took it.

My issue with evacuation is primarily my dog, a ninety-pound Rottweiler named Dorian. I'm well aware that, in an emergency evacuation situation, he would not be allowed to come with me. So I always have to make a decision based on him. I always prefer to stay in my home. I mean, I guess I'm bourgeois in that regard. My home is my refuge and I feel safe there.

I've been getting collateral eyewitness reports, different information since I evacuated. But yesterday, I had an actual phone conversation with one of my neighbors, and our block did not flood all that greatly. My house didn't have any interior water, but I do apparently have some roof damage. So I'll be making a roof claim, but not a flood claim. *(Dorian barks in background.)*

Okay. There is Dorian making his presence known. Speaking of water, he must need some.

Water is kind of an omnipresent theme in New Orleans—our relationship with the waters that surround us. We realize, on one level, that we live in a precarious situation. But even beyond that, the river is just this powerful force. You actually feel its strength if you're standing on the levee. When I say it's an omnipresent theme, I mean being surrounded by water, and knowing that most of the city lies below. And that there've been significant floods in history that have devastated the city. But yet people keep coming back.

As with everything in New Orleans, it's extremes. There's that sense of danger—that once water starts flowing, it's seeking its level and there's nothing you can do. But there's also an immense beauty and strength to the river. So you respect it like this living thing. And water is what people make their livelihoods on in New Orleans—fishing, the river, offshore. The dampness of the air affects your life.

The musician Dr. John says water even affects the music, because with the amount of moisture that's in the air at any given point, sound waves travel better. Thunder in New Orleans is the most incredible sound I've ever heard. It goes on forever. It can be abrupt and booming and you can hear it echoing on and on.

So anyway, on Sunday afternoon, we started off. We arrived in Memphis in the wee hours of Monday morning. Checked into a roach motel. Had to put ourselves on a waiting list. Stayed in the roach motel for about a day and a half. Katrina passed over us that night.

By that point, we knew things were bad. So we were just kind of hanging out in the hotel room playing spades, you know, just trying to just chill out. It was a lot of rain,

[left to right] Esquizito Paul Perez (evacuee), Dorian (Esquizito's beloved dog), Linda Cronin-Gross (host)

even in Memphis. From there, we went to Bowling Green, Kentucky. Stayed with some friends for a few days in this very spacious kind of suburban, once-rural area. Very peaceful. Went to Atlanta. That's where we started to kind of splinter off. I stayed with some friends for about a week and a half. It was in Atlanta that I went online and found HurricaneHousing.

I responded to thirty-five different host opportunities. One of them was Linda. Linda offered a guestroom so I wouldn't be displacing anybody else. There's a door on the room, which appealed to me 'cause I knew I would need some solitude and privacy. I lived by myself in New Orleans. I used to live in New York, on the west side of Manhattan, Hell's Kitchen. I just knew instinctively that, for what I was going through, Brooklyn would be better for me than even my old neighborhood.

LINDA CRONIN-GROSS: We're here in Sunset Park, Brooklyn. I've had people stay in the guestroom. This is a three-story brownstone and on the top floor, I have a business, a small PR firm. My company, LCG Communications, have clients like Sustainable South Bronx, New York Lawyers for the Public Interest. Neighborhood Housing Services of New York City, which is probably our biggest client. So you get the drift. We do communications for not-for-profits and progressive grassroots groups in the New York City. I always tell people if they wanna see how we're spending their money, they can see that we're not spending it on fancy offices.

To tell you the truth, I didn't think many people from New Orleans would want to come all the way to New York City. But I figured I'd put it up there because it wouldn't really be a big deal to have an extra person around. It's like a small sitcom here anyway, people are in and out all day. I have three, four employees, a cat and two children. I live with my daughter, Amanda, who's fifteen. I have a son too, but he's twenty-three, so he comes back to do stuff like laundry. Then there is the staff. They're here from nine-to-five, Monday through Friday. So, one more person, honestly, didn't seem like that big of deal. Plus, everybody felt like they wanted to do something. Watching those pictures was very scary.

I blog occasionally for the Huffington Post. Right after Katrina, that's all anybody could talk about online. What else are you supposed to be talking about as a major American city is being left to collapse?

So I had blogged about how Cuba does this better and it's the truth. No matter what you think about Cuba or Fidel Castro, they get people out of the way of hurricanes regularly. They literally moved over one-and-a-half-million people out of the way of their last hurricane without one death, because they have a plan. I decided to just blog that. So it came back at me. I had some good comments. But there were also a lot of the "freepers." There's a site called Free Republicans Online on the blog, and as soon as you put "Cuba" in the title, it attracts them like sharks to blood in the water. So I got all of these really nasty posts, which is fine. I always feel like that means at least people are reading it.

One of the things that also came up on some of the left-wing posts was this whole chant saying: "Stop pointing fingers," and "Do something besides complain." So I said, "Well, all right." I knew that MoveOn was doing the HurricaneHousing site. First of all, it was a great idea and I'm not just saying that 'cause I'm a member. What really amazed me is that a lot of people who had very little to offer were offering it anyway. There were people saying, "I have a couch. I can double up with my daughter in her room." People were offering floors or a mattress thrown on a floor. People who clearly couldn't even afford to do this or who were already in cramped situations, from all over the country. So I said, "Well, this is a cool thing to be part of." The rest is history, I guess.

ESQUIZITO: I've felt so fortunate and lucky. It's been wonderful. A couple of weeks ago, there was a full moon and I sat out in the yard here, talking on my cell phone to folks. It's really been great. I have everything I need.

But I have to say that there's nothing like your own pillow, particularly in a situation like this. I've been in situations where I've been on tour, and it's different because you know when you're going back home.

LINDA: Esquizito just kind of blended in seamlessly. Of course, he has made great efforts to do his own thing, trying not to push himself into everything. He's been very good about that. He's been very aware of not always being the focus of attention. I appreciate that. We always said if it didn't look like it was working out, we'd shake hands and it would be over. But it's working out fine.

My daughter's having a little issue with the dog. She's never had a dog. So we're working that out. The pets themselves, of course, had their own issues. I have a cat, Star. But the cat and the dog, they've worked it out.

ESQUIZITO: Yeah. Linda has been very generous and very welcoming. …

LINDA: What else is he gonna say, sitting next to me? (*Laughter*)

ESQUIZITO: What's more, she understands. I think she has a very keen sense of what this means, what I'm going through. She's out of her mind, you know, which is something that's always appealed to me.

LINDA: Wow! That's a backhanded compliment. (*Laughs*)

ESQUIZITO: And we just seemed to develop a connection very early on.

LINDA: I think it also helps that I actually have—not like Esquizito, Esquizito does it professionally—but I do have

sort of an interesting past, which includes a very short-lived career in music. I was in a punk band. When punk was new. The late '70s. We were like a C-list band. It was called Uncle Son, named after a Kinks song, which has great lyrics. We hung out at CBGB's; we played some other venues. I remember all the clubs. It was a very interesting time. When you had to actually step over people 'cause it was on the Bowery. It was a semi-scary experience getting into CBGB's back then. It was a little pre-Ramones and Debbie Harry and all that stuff. But it was fun until it wasn't anymore. So I have some appreciation of what musicians need to go through.

I was also an elementary school teacher. Both private and in the city school system for about seven years. I grew up in Queens. Can you tell? I made a little bit of an effort to flatten out my accent, but I can hear it the whole time, and I'm like, *my God.*

ESQUIZITO: I grew up in Los Angeles. I was the only one in my family not born in Los Angeles. My family's an old New Orleans, Seventh Ward Creole family. I went to music school in Boston, Berkelee College of Music. When I lived in New York, from like '85 to '98, I did music and I also did social service. I was not trained in social service,

but it was the '80s, you know, spelled with a capital A, so I just fell into doing AIDS education, social health education. Which later segued into doing violence prevention, life skills type of work. Mostly using art and interactive learning to teach.

Going from city to city, adjusting—re-adjusting—to the New York pace of life and how people interact with each other here, that's been challenging to me. The city has changed, but I think I've changed more. I think New Orleans had a lot to do with that. Being back in New York, after living in New Orleans, I literally ask myself: *Did I ever live here?* I've just gotten so used to walking out my door and seeing old oak trees and colorful old houses, that now when I go into Manhattan, I just think, *What planet have I fallen on here?*

New Orleans is a very spiritually charged place. There are things that happen day in and day out that you don't really question. Some of us don't feel complete without the city of New Orleans. Now there are things that are probably lost forever. Like Horace's Bar. It's on the uptown second line parade route. It's just one of these places where I'd start playing with the second line and roll for about half an hour and once we hit that bar it was the perfect place to stop and rest. You know, just after the storm hit—that would have been the start of the second line season. About every Sunday till the holidays, there's a second line parade.

We would just march and dance and play the music… but now there's nobody there. It's ghostly. That's a significant loss. That's one of the things that completely existed outside the New Orleans that's geared for the tourists. It's for the people that lived in those neighborhoods.

A second line parade is different from a Mardi Gras parade. Mardi Gras parades are big public spectacles, open to the public. A second line is a street parade enacted by and for the people in the community.

The term "second line" refers to the uninvited participants in a jazz funeral. A hundred and fifty years ago, you'd hire a brass band to play hymns and dirges for funerals, so it comes from the tradition of a jazz funeral procession. It's a chance for folks to have their own thing,

not meant for visitors or outsiders or tourists. They're for working-class black folks and most of them roll through the neighborhoods. People hear the music coming and go meet the band. Thus they were referred to as the "second line," the first line being the funeral musicians, the second line being those not invited. That's the official story, but really it just allowed people here to have a party.

Ultimately, it turned into a social event. After the band played the funeral music, they'd play more joyous music for the second line folk. If you heard a brass band coming down the street, you'd stop what you were doing and follow them. Louis Armstrong talks of following the second line as a child. For a kid, it was the most exciting thing that could happen. Musicians were idols of the community; they had power and influence. The music they played was new, and evolving right before their eyes.

These days it's a community social event sponsored by the Social Aid and Pleasure clubs—black benevolent societies which function primarily for health and burial insurance. Because of segregation, black folks had to come up with their own institutions, so the Social Aid and Pleasure clubs were groups of individuals set up to help communities. They were the activist organizations of their day, with, of course, a party element. These days they exist to provide a community outlet and for the preservation of a way of life and heritage. Today, they are groups of folks that sponsor parades for social and historical reasons.

It's become an annual or seasonal thing, but now… those neighborhoods are destroyed. With no neighborhoods or people, it's difficult to have a parade. As I said, it's a significant loss.

It's been an intense year in New Orleans. Tootie Montana, last June, died while giving testimony in front of the City Council. There was a special session to address what happened on what's called Super Sunday. Super Sunday is around St. Joseph's Day and it's one of the traditions for the Mardi Gras Indians. It's the only day other than Mardi Gras that you'll see Indians on the street. And there was some police harassment. Tootie got up to testify, and he's speaking from over fifty years experience as an Indian. He's recounting how this happened routinely when he was younger, the police harassment, and his last words were: "This has got to stop." And then he had a heart attack.

Tootie's funeral was intense. Up until the storm, it was probably the most intense experience I've had in New Orleans. And that whole culture is gone, for the moment. It's going to take a while for it to come back in any form that resembles what it was before August 29th. Because it needs the people. It's not simply the bands of musicians; it's the whole experience. On a Sunday afternoon, people who don't have much at all come out and parade. Now there's no one in those neighborhoods to do it. But I know they'll return.

Some of the greatest music this country has ever manifested has come out of immense hardship. That's ostensibly the story of jazz. Even before emancipation, blacks in New Orleans, on Sundays, could go to this area of town where they had an experience of freedom—or at least a feeling of freedom—through music and dance and social activity. That can't possibly happen right now. All those neighborhoods have been devastated.

Life is tenuous in New Orleans and always has been. It's precarious; it's often hard and full of neglect. And in response to that people look for beauty and joy and a full experience of life.

I could return to my home now. It still stands. It stood there for almost 150 years. But I'm waiting. I don't trust New Orleans city officials, Louisiana State officials or U.S. government officials to do right with the city of New Orleans. I'm waiting for more on-the-ground eyewitness reports of people that I can trust.

This event is the most defining circumstance in this country since the Civil War. It lifted all of these veils. America tells the world we're the greatest country on the face of the earth. But what are they gauging greatness by, if not ability to manage citizens and societies?

For those of us who realize what's needed and have ideas of how to make a better society, the further questions are: What can we achieve now? How can we make a difference in the larger institutions? How do we mount a real revolution?

Do we throw away our government institutions and say, "They're never gonna serve us in the way we need to be served, so don't even look"? Or do we say, "Well, wait a minute, what are we all paying for here"? That's the larger issue of Katrina and America right now—this sense of democracy that's being destroyed simply because a lot of people feel powerless to actually make an impact.

LINDA: The government has failed us in a way that I didn't even think they could fail us. I never thought I'd see people floating dead down the streets of a major American city.

ESQUIZITO: As a musician, I play mostly solo, but to make your way both creatively and financially, people usually have two or three different projects. Some friends of mine put together this New Orleans benefit, readings and music. Readings of just regular folks, of officials, of emails, interspersed with music. So we're all doing what we can. Right now I'm just checking out the New York scene again, going to different open mics, jam sessions, meeting some musicians that I've wanted to meet for a long time.

I booked a gig in November, which will probably turn out to be my thank you and farewell New York concert. I'm shooting for returning to New Orleans for Thanksgiving, which is actually my anniversary. Dorian and I left New York in 1998 and thirty-six hours later, arrived in New Orleans. Thanksgiving morning 1998. So come Thanksgiving I'll be gone. Because the music for me is in New Orleans.

I know some people are saying, "I can't come back now." But if you love music and you love the spirit and soul of New Orleans, now is a historic time.

Everywhere you look there's a potential heartbreak and that's a negotiation, too. How much heartbreak do you try to avoid and how much do you meet on its own terms? I think musicians back in New Orleans now will have this immense desire to make the best music they can possibly make—to make it as beautiful as you possibly can in response to the horror of the situation.

That's all we can do: try to meet that horror with the same amount of beauty. ⇨

HURRICANE KATRINA: THE SECOND CRISIS

By James Rucker, Executive Director, Color of Change.org

The stories in this book are a window into an unprecedented moment in American history—a moment where a massive human tragedy was met with a massive opening of our homes and our hearts. They remind us that, in the face of the horrors we saw unfold on the Gulf Coast, Americans responded with compassion and kindness. We really *were* good. But for too many of those whose lives were uprooted and overturned by Hurricane Katrina, the horrors of those first awful weeks in the fall of 2005 have given way to new fears, new struggles and new displacements.

One year after the hurricane, hundreds of thousands of Katrina survivors (including many of those featured in this book) are still struggling. Many are not much better off than they were immediately after Katrina arrived; some are arguably worse off. They are trying to rebuild their lives, to prevent the loss of their battered homes, to find jobs and to take care of their children. Despite the initial outpouring of support, those who were left behind in August, 2005 find themselves on the verge of being left behind again. This is the second crisis of Katrina.

How did it come to this? Why, when our individual actions exemplified such deep empathy and compassion, has our collective response fallen so short? Why, when we did so much as individuals to knit a fabric of community around those who lost everything, do we find our national safety net in such tatters?

Our government bears a large share of the responsibility. The collective extension of our individual values of care and compassion, of our fierce sense of responsibility to our neighbors, be they next door or thousands of miles away, is the safety net of government services that we entrust with taking care of those Americans most at risk. Through Katrina, we got a terrifying look at the health of that safety net.

We can blame our leaders, but it would be disserving and dishonest to stop there. We must acknowledge that we bear responsibility when the performance of our democratically elected government falls short of our values. We bear responsibility when our government's actions deviate from our vision of ourselves as an empathetic and compassionate people.

Averting the second crisis of Katrina will not be accomplished by individual acts of compassion; it will only be accomplished by collective acts of civic and political engagement. Standing by those left behind in the aftermath of Katrina means paying attention to initiatives that directly address rebuilding and recovery in the Gulf. It means being on the lookout for legislation that, under the guise of making room in the budget for the costs of the rebuild, cuts social programs for all Americans. It means speaking out against national or local actions that undermine survivors' chances of returning home, or that fail to support them in starting over elsewhere.

Standing up for our democracy means attending to more than the Gulf. This second crisis calls for deep and longstanding engagement, for a personal commitment. It requires letting our representatives know that they have our support when they choose to serve those in need and letting them hear our disapproval when they choose not to. It means participating in our democracy as if others' lives depended on it. Because they do.

As the rest of the story of Hurricane Katrina is written, I hope that it will not just be about Americans at our best, but about America at its best. America *can be* great because Americans are good. But America *won't* be great unless we make it so through our actions. Here's hoping we can each step up to the challenge. ⇨

At the time of publication, there were several organizations doing work to hold government accountable and restore the lives of those displaced by Katrina. To learn more, volunteer or provide financial support, visit the following websites:

Katrina Action
http://www.katrinaaction.org/

The People's Hurricane Relief Fund
http://www.communitylaborunited.net/

Common Ground Relief
http://www.commongroundrelief.org/

NAACP
http://www.naacp.org/

ACORN *(Association of Community Organizations for Reform Now)*
http://www.acorn.org/

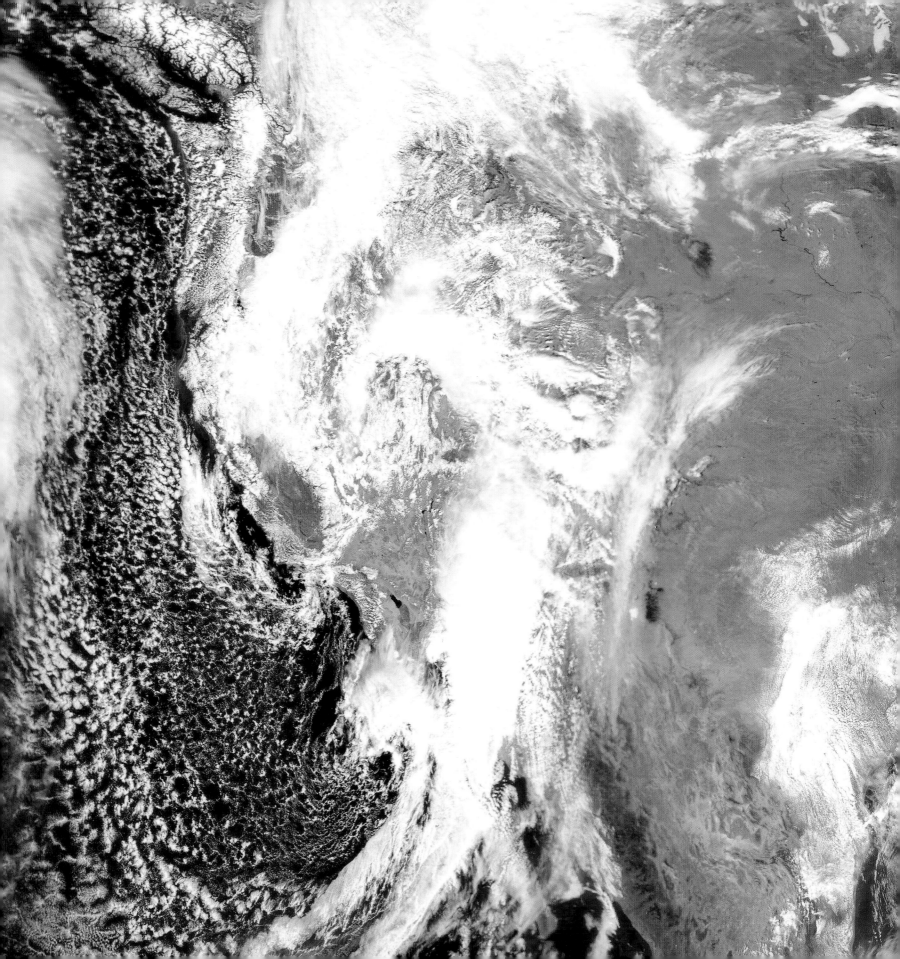

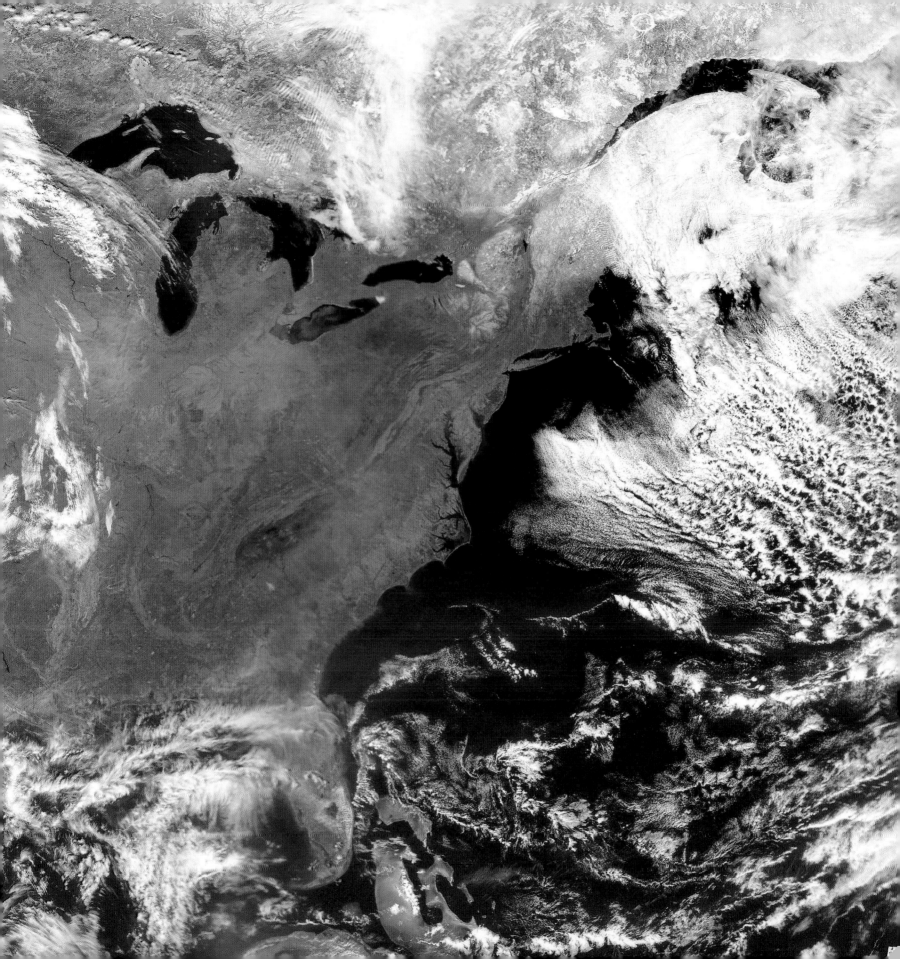

ACKNOWLEDGMENTS

Thanks to everyone who helped with HurricaneHousing. org—the staff, the volunteers, the organizations and news outlets, and especially the brave and wonderful people who opened their homes and made it all possible.

Special thanks must go to the courageous evacuees who took the time, in the midst of so much turmoil, to share their stories with us.

Thank you to: Tanya Africa, Micayla Birondo, Joan Blades, Wes Boyd, Ben Brandzel, Namrita Chaudhary, Matt Ewing, Randall Farmer, Adam Green, Patrick Michael Kane, Rosalyn Lemieux, Jennifer Lindenauer, Tom Matzzie, Carrie Olson, Erik Olson, Marika Olson, Eli Pariser, Aaron Ross, Adam Ruben, Justin Ruben, James Rucker, Rob Starkey and Noah Winer.

Todd Shuster and everyone at Zachary Shuster Harmsworth.

Mark Huntley, Bernardo Issel, Daron Murphy, Pete Nelson, Annie Nocenti, Sabin Streeter, Jeffrey Witte, Senator Barack Obama, Kate Babkirk, Nick Allen of Donor Digital; the MoveOn volunteer transcribing team (Ross Barentyne-Truluck, Lynn Cole, Allison Hastings, Alf Maglalang, Edward Mayo, & Alex Orban); Lisa Fitzpatrick, Linda Kelly, Iain Morris, Cree McCree, and everyone at Palace Press; Ira Arlook, Simon Aronoff, David Fenton, Trevor Fitzgibbon, Alex Howe, Kawana Lloyd, Jessica Smith, Steve Smith and everyone at Fenton Communications; Steven Kest and everyone at ACORN, Ella St. Clair, Barbara Dozier, Rebecca Hill, Chris & Sharon Meinke, Shannon Strathmann, John Cusack, Tim Robbins, Moby, Rosie Perez, The Roots, Green Day, Pearl Jam, R.E.M., the Black Eyed Peas, the Beastie Boys, 311, John Mellencamp, Vanessa Carlton, Stephen Jenkins, Liz Phair, Dino Meneghin, Meredith Fitzgibbon, Carol Plummer, Joshua Kahn, Princess Allan,

Shania Allan, Mary L. Froning, everyone at the NAACP, Melissa Williams and Daniel Mintz; Geof Cahoon, Lisa Jebsen, Ellen Prusinski and all of the other volunteers who helped review posts and deal with hundreds of HurricaneHousing. org questions from other hosts and evacuees; the folks at KatrinaHousing.com and other volunteer-run sites who did an incredible job housing thousands more people just like the ones featured in this book and who helped direct evacuees to our postings; everyone at TrueMajority.com; Bill Zimmerman, Pacy Markman, Matt Durning, Susan Fairbairn, Elvia Gaitan, Roberta Green, Andrew Halpern, Pat Sheffield, and everyone at Zimmerman and Markman; Andrew Halpern, Mark Medernarch, Jiannjyh Chen, Melissa Timme and everyone at DUCK Studios; Getty Images, John Kerry and everyone at JohnKerry.com; Tom Anderson, Bich Ngoc Cao, Chris DeWolfe, Matt Polesetsky, Lucas Buck and everyone at MySpace.com, MeetUp.com, DemocracyForAmerica.com, BlueLatinos.org, PlusThree.com and DonorDigital.org.

Special thanks to Andy and Deborah Rappaport, whose generous support made the 1-800 hotline possible; to Becky Bond, Beth Dalton, and the whole team at Working Assets; and to the staff and operators at UpSource, Inc. who went way above and beyond the call of duty to set up and run the 1-800 hotline.

And to C. B. Smith, for his amazing photographs.

Thanks also to HurricaneHousing.com (who run their own website selling hurricane-proof shelters) for pointing folks our way for the duration of the project.

—**Laura Dawn, Cultural Director**
MoveOn.org Civic Action ⇨